SIMPLE CHINESE COOKERY

SIMPLE CHINESE COOKERY

KEN
HOM

Step by step to
everyone's favourite
Chinese recipes

BBC
BOOKS

About the author

Ken Hom is widely regarded as one of the world's greatest authorities on oriental cooking. He has made several series for the BBC including *Hot Wok*, *Travels with a Hot Wok* and *Foolproof Chinese Cookery*, and his many books are worldwide bestsellers. He is a director of Noble House Leisure Limited, which includes the Yellow River Cafés and other restaurants, and lives in London, Paris, south-west France and Bangkok.

Food photography by Jean Cazals

The hardback edition of this book, *Foolproof Chinese Cookery*, was published to accompany the television series Foolproof Chinese Cookery which was produced for the BBC by Independent Image Ltd.

Series Producer/Director for Independent Image Ltd: Kate Kinninmont.

Published by BBC Books,
BBC Worldwide Ltd,
Woodlands,
80 Wood Lane,
London W12 0TT

First published in hardback as *Foolproof Chinese Cookery*
This paperback edition first published in 2005
Copyright © Promo Group Ltd 2000
The moral right of Ken Hom to be identified as the author of this work has been asserted.

Food photography © Jean Cazals 2000

ISBN 0 563 52179 1

Commissioning editor: Vivien Bowler
Project editor: Lara Speicher
Copy editor: Jane Middleton
Art direction: Lisa Pettibone
Designers: Norma Martin and Lisa Pettibone
Home economist: Linda Tubby
Stylist: Sue Rowlands
Production controller: Arlene Alexander

The publishers would like to thank the following for supplying items used in the photographs: David Mellor, Divertimenti, Gong, Kara Kara and Yves Ogier.

Set in Univers
Printed and bound in Italy by LEGO SpA
Colour separations by Wyndeham Kestrel, Witham

Contents

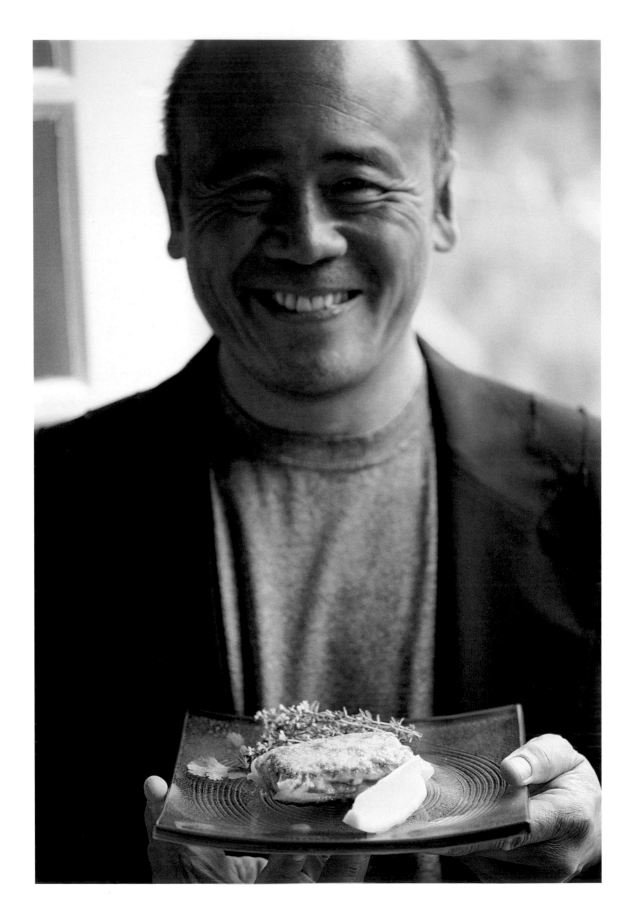

Introduction

My knowledge and love of Chinese cookery came from watching and imitating chefs at my uncle's restaurant, where I was a young apprentice. Later, as a culinary professor, I was struck by the fact that although many of my students had read about various techniques in one or more of the many fine Chinese cookbooks available, it was only when they saw them demonstrated that they really understood them. And only then could they attempt to duplicate what I had shown them. The step-by-step procedures that I developed became the basis of my teaching and I used them extensively as a broadcaster. They form the backbone of the recipes in this book. The cliché about pictures being worth a thousand words is more valid than ever.

China has one of the world's oldest culinary traditions. Its cuisine is unique because it developed independently of the West. Because of the ancient, insular civilization, poor transportation network, lack of arable land, shortage of fuels and lack of ovens, Chinese chefs were forced to accommodate their art to necessity. Later, as the Chinese moved abroad, they took this culinary heritage with them. If one wishes to understand the essence of Chinese cooking, therefore, it is important to make a cultural leap of faith.

Chinese cooks are engaged in creating harmony. The size and shape of the food, the fragrances and the contrasting tastes and textures are all part of the final result. Our aim is to attain a balance between all these elements. Often when I demonstrate, people are surprised by the simplicity and logic of this ancient cuisine. The tools we use are remarkably few and simple and the techniques so effective that cooks from other cuisines now use many of them.

In this book, you will see that Chinese cooking is really not very complex. The step-by-step photographs and the thoroughly tested recipes will help you to achieve success. However, you should be bold. Trust your palate. Follow the techniques and recipes but feel free to add your own touches. Adjust, invent, as Chinese cooks have done for centuries. Incorporate your favourite Chinese ingredients when cooking dishes from other cuisines. Use the techniques that you have mastered from this book and build upon them.

It is my hope that the pleasure you gain from making these foolproof recipes will give you the confidence of a true Chinese cook.

'Chinese cooks are engaged in creating harmony. The size and shape of the food, the fragrances and the contrasting tastes and textures are all part of the final result.'

Ingredients and Equipment

INGREDIENTS

Events of the past few decades have opened up the kitchens of the world to Asian food, and many of the most exotic ingredients are now readily available in the West. This is especially true of Chinese food. The following is a brief guide to ingredients used in this book.

Beancurd

Also known by its Chinese name, *doufu*, or the Japanese, tofu, beancurd is highly nutritious and rich in protein, with a distinctive texture but bland taste. It is made from yellow soya beans, which are soaked, ground, mixed with water and then cooked briefly before being solidified. Beancurd is readily available in two forms – as firm cakes or as a thickish junket – and may also be found in several dried forms and in a fermented version. The soft junket-like variety (sometimes called silken tofu) is used for soups, while the solid type is used for stir-frying, braising and poaching. Solid beancurd 'cakes' are white in colour and are sold in supermarkets and Chinese grocers, as well as in many healthfood shops. They are packed in water in plastic containers and may be kept in this state in the refrigerator for up to five days, provided the water is changed daily.

To use solid beancurd, cut it into cubes or shreds with a sharp knife. Do this with care as it is delicate. It also needs to be cooked carefully, as too much stirring can cause it to crumble.

Bok Choy
(Chinese White Cabbage)

Although there are many varieties, the most common bok choy is the one with a long, smooth, milky-white stem and large, crinkly, dark-green leaves. The smaller the plant, the more tender it will be. Bok choy has a light, fresh, slightly mustardy flavour and requires little cooking. It is now widely available in supermarkets. Look for firm, crisp stalks and unblemished leaves. Store bok choy in the vegetable crisper of your refrigerator.

Caul Fat

Caul fat is a lacy membrane that lines the stomach cavity of pigs and cows. It melts during cooking and is often used by European and Chinese cooks to encase stuffings and keep meat moist and delicious. You should be able to order caul fat from your local butcher. It is highly perishable, so buy it in small quantities and use quickly. For longer storage, wrap the caul fat carefully and freeze it. To defrost, rinse in cold water. I find that soaking caul fat in cold water before use helps to separate the fat without tearing its lacy, fragile webs.

Chillies

Chillies are used extensively in western China, less so in the south. They are the seed pods of capsicum plants and can be obtained fresh, dried or ground. There are many types available and they vary greatly in flavour and heat.

Fresh Chillies

Fresh chillies should look fresh and bright, with no brown patches or black spots. As a general rule, red chillies are milder than green ones because they sweeten as they ripen, but nevertheless some red chillies can be very spicy indeed.

To prepare fresh chillies, rinse them in cold water, then slit them lengthways with a small sharp knife. Remove and discard the seeds. Rinse the chillies again under cold running water and then prepare them according to the recipe. Wash your hands, knife and chopping board before preparing other foods, and be careful not to touch your eyes until you have washed your hands thoroughly.

Dried Red Chillies

The dried red chillies used in China are usually small, thin and about 1 cm (½ in) long. They are normally left whole or cut in half lengthways with the seeds left in and used to season oil for stir-fried dishes, sauces and braises.

The Chinese like to blacken them and leave them in the dish during cooking but, as they are extremely hot, you may prefer to remove them immediately after using them to flavour the cooking oil. They can be found in Chinese and Asian grocers as well as in most supermarkets and will keep indefinitely in a tightly covered jar. When eating out, most diners carefully move the blackened chillies to one side of their plate.

Chilli Oil/Chilli Dipping Sauce

Chilli oil is sometimes used as a dipping condiment as well as a seasoning in China. It varies in strength according to the chillies used. The Thai and Malaysian versions are especially hot, the Taiwanese and Chinese ones more subtle. Commercial oils are quite acceptable but the home-made version is best, so I have included a recipe below. Remember that chilli oil is too intense to be used as the sole cooking oil, so combine it with milder oils. This recipe includes pepper and black beans for additional flavours so it can also be used as a dipping sauce.

Green and red fresh chillies; dried red chillies

150 ml (5 fl oz) groundnut oil
2 tablespoons chopped dried red chillies
1 tablespoon unroasted Sichuan
   peppercorns
2 tablespoons whole salted black beans

Heat a wok over a high heat, then add the oil followed by all the rest of the ingredients. Cook over a low heat for about 10 minutes, then remove from the heat and leave to cool. Pour into a jar and leave for 2 days, then strain the oil. Store in a tightly sealed glass jar in a cool, dark place, where it will keep indefinitely.

Chilli Powder

Chilli powder is made from dried red chillies and is used in many spicy dishes. As with chillies in general, add it according to taste.

Chinese Flowering Cabbage

Chinese flowering cabbage, or choi sum, is part of the mustard green cabbage family. It has green leaves and may have small yellow flowers, which can be eaten along with the leaves and stems. In China this is one of the most popular leafy vegetables and makes a delicious stir-fry dish.

Clockwise from top left: pak choy, chinese flowering cabbage, coriander, bok choy

Chinese Leaves (Peking Cabbage)

This delicious, crunchy vegetable comes in various sizes, from long, compact, barrel-shaped ones to short, squat types. The heads are tightly packed with firm, pale-green (or in some cases slightly yellow), crinkled leaves. It is most commonly added to soups and meat stir-fries but its ability to absorb flavours and its pleasant taste and texture make it a favourite with chefs, who match it with rich foods. Store it as you would ordinary cabbage.

Coriander (Chinese Parsley)

Fresh coriander is one of the relatively few herbs used in Chinese cookery. It looks like flat-leaf parsley but its pungent, musky, citrus-like flavour gives it a distinctive character that is unmistakable. Its delicate leaves are often used as a garnish, or they can be chopped and mixed into sauces and stuffings. Parsley can be substituted, although the taste will not be the same.

When buying fresh coriander, choose deep-green leaves; limp, yellowing leaves indicate age and should be avoided. To store coriander,

wash it in cold water, dry thoroughly (preferably in a salad spinner) and wrap in kitchen paper. Put it in the vegetable compartment of your refrigerator, where it should keep for several days.

Cornflour

In China there are many flours and types of starch, such as water chestnut powder, taro starch and arrowroot. They are primarily used to bind ingredients together, thicken sauces and make batters. These exotic starches and flours are difficult to obtain outside China but I have found that cornflour works just as well in my recipes. Used in marinades, it helps to coat the food properly and it gives dishes a velvety texture. It also protects food during deep-frying by helping to seal in the juices, and can be used as a binder in minced stuffings. Before adding cornflour to sauces, blend it to a smooth paste with a little cold water. During cooking, the cornflour paste will turn clear and shiny.

Egg White

In Chinese recipes, egg whites are often used in batters and as a coating to seal in the food's flavour and juices when it is plunged into hot oil. It is especially important in velveting – a technique where chicken is coated in egg white and cornflour, then blanched in oil or water. One large egg white is about 2 tablespoons. You can easily freeze raw egg whites in tablespoon-size cubes in an ice-cube tray.

Five-spice Powder

Also known as five-flavoured powder or five-fragrance spice powder, this is becoming a staple in the spice section of supermarkets, and Chinese grocers always keep it in stock. It is a mixture of ground star anise, Sichuan peppercorns, fennel, cloves and cinnamon. A good blend will be pungent, fragrant, spicy and slightly sweet. The exotic fragrance it gives to a dish makes the search for good five-spice powder well worth the effort. It keeps indefinitely in a tightly sealed jar.

Garlic

Garlic has been an essential seasoning in Chinese cookery for thousands of years. Indeed, Chinese food would be unrecognizable without its highly aromatic smell and

Garlic and ginger

distinctive taste. It is used to flavour oils as well as spicy sauces and is often paired with other pungent ingredients, such as spring onions, black beans and fresh ginger.

Select bulbs of garlic that are firm and preferably pinkish in colour. Store in a cool, dry place but not in the refrigerator, where it can easily become mildewed or start sprouting.

Ginger

Fresh root ginger is an indispensable ingredient in Chinese cooking. Its pungent, spicy taste adds a subtle but distinctive flavour to soups, meats and vegetables and it is also an important seasoning for fish and seafood, since it neutralizes fishy smells.

Root ginger looks rather like a gnarled Jerusalem artichoke and can vary in length from 7.5–15 cm (3–6 in). Select firm, unshrivelled pieces and peel off the skin before use. It will keep in the refrigerator, well wrapped in clingfilm, for about two weeks. Dried powdered ginger has a quite different flavour and should not be substituted for fresh.

Most of the recipes in this book that require ginger specify that it should be finely shredded or chopped. For shredded ginger, thinly slice a piece lengthways, then stack and cut lengthways again into fine strips. To chop finely, turn the shredded ginger round and chop it horizontally.

Ham

Chinese ham has a rich, salty flavour and is used primarily as a garnish or seasoning for soups, sauces, stir-fries, noodles and rice. Parma ham or lean English smoked bacon (with any rind or fat cut away) makes a good substitute.

Mangetout (Snow Peas)

This familiar vegetable combines a tender, crunchy texture with a sweet, fresh flavour. Look for firm pods with very small peas, which means they are tender and young. Mangetout should keep for about a week in the vegetable crisper of the refrigerator.

Mushrooms

Chinese Dried Mushrooms

There are many varieties of these, either black or brown, but the very large, pale ones with a

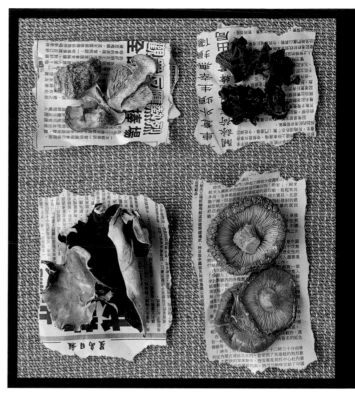

Clockwise from top left: straw mushrooms, tree fungus, Chinese dried mushrooms, wood ear fungus

cracked surface are the best. They are usually the most expensive, so use them sparingly. They are available in boxes or plastic bags from Chinese grocers. Store in an airtight jar.

To use dried mushrooms, soak them in a bowl of warm water for about 20 minutes or until they are soft and pliable. Squeeze out the excess water, then cut off and discard the woody stems. Only the caps should be used. The soaking water can be saved and used in soups or for cooking rice. Strain it through a fine sieve to discard any sand or residue from the dried mushrooms.

Chinese Tree Fungus

These tiny, black, dried leaves are also known as cloud ears, because when soaked they puff up like little clouds. They are valued for their crunchy texture and slightly smoky flavour. You should be able to find them at Chinese markets, usually wrapped in plastic bags. They keep indefinitely in a jar stored in a cool, dry place. Before use, soak them in hot water for 20–30 minutes until soft, then rinse well, cutting away any hard bits.

Chinese Wood Ear Fungus

This is a larger variety of the Chinese tree fungus described on the previous page. Soak and trim them in the same manner before use. During soaking, they will swell up to four or five times their original size. They keep indefinitely when stored in a jar in a cool dry place.

Straw Mushrooms

These are among the tastiest mushrooms to be found in China. When fresh they have deep brown caps which are moulded around the stem. In the West they are only available in tins, from Chinese grocers and some supermarkets and delicatessens. Drain and rinse in cold water before use.

Noodles

In China, people eat noodles (pasta) of all kinds, day and night, in restaurants and at food stalls. They provide a nutritious, quick, light snack and are usually of good quality. Several types of Chinese noodles have now made their way into the West.

Clockwise from top left: flat wheat noodles, beanthread noodles, egg noodles, rice noodles, round wheat noodles

Bean Thread (Transparent) Noodles

Also called cellophane noodles, these very fine, white noodles are made from ground mung beans. They are available dried, packed in neat, plastic-wrapped bundles, from Chinese markets and supermarkets.

Bean thread noodles are never served on their own but are added to soups or braises or deep-fried and used as a garnish. Soak them in warm water for about 5 minutes before use. As they are rather long, you might find it easier to cut them into shorter lengths after soaking. If you are frying them, they do not need soaking beforehand but they do need to be separated. The best way to do this is to pull them apart in a large paper bag, which stops them flying all over the place.

Rice Noodles

These dried noodles are opaque white and come in a variety of shapes and thicknesses. One of the most common is rice stick noodles, which are flat and about the length of a chopstick. Rice noodles are very easy to prepare. Simply soak them in warm water for 20 minutes until they are soft, then drain in a colander or sieve. They are now ready to be used in soups or stir-fried.

Wheat Noodles and Egg Noodles

Available dried or fresh, these are made from hard or soft wheat flour, water, and sometimes egg, in which case they are labelled egg noodles. Flat noodles are usually used in soups, while rounded ones are best for frying. The fresh ones freeze well if they are tightly wrapped. Thaw thoroughly before cooking.

Dried wheat or fresh egg noodles are very good blanched and served as an accompaniment to main dishes instead of plain rice. If you are cooking noodles ahead of time or before stir-frying them, toss the cooked, drained noodles in 2 teaspoons of sesame oil and put them into a bowl. Cover this with clingfilm and refrigerate for up to 2 hours.

Oils

Oil is the most commonly used cooking medium in China, although animal fats, usually lard and chicken fat, are also used in some areas, particularly in the north.

To re-use oil after deep-frying, let it cool, then filter it through muslin or a fine sieve into a jar. Seal and store in a cool, dry place. If you keep it in the refrigerator it will become cloudy, but it will clarify again when it returns to room temperature. I find oils are best re-used just once, which is healthier, since their saturated fat content increases the more you use them.

Groundnut Oil

This is also known as peanut or arachide oil. I prefer to use it for Chinese cookery because it has a pleasant, unobtrusive taste. Although it has a higher saturated fat content than some oils, its ability to be heated to a high temperature without burning makes it perfect for stir-frying and deep-frying. Most supermarkets stock groundnut oil but if you cannot find it, use corn oil instead.

Corn Oil

Corn or maize oil is also quite suitable for Chinese cooking, since it has a high heating point. However, I find it rather bland and with a slightly disagreeable smell. It is high in polyunsaturates and is therefore one of the healthier oils.

Other Vegetable Oils

Some of the cheaper vegetable oils available include soya bean, safflower and sunflower. Light in colour and taste, they can be used in Chinese cooking but take care, since they smoke and burn at lower temperatures than groundnut oil.

Sesame Oil

This thick, rich, golden brown oil made from sesame seeds has a distinctive, nutty flavour and aroma. It is widely used in Chinese cookery as a seasoning but is not normally used as a cooking oil because it burns easily. Think of it more as a flavouring than a cooking oil. A small amount is often added at the last moment to finish a dish.

Peanuts

Raw peanuts are widely used in Chinese cooking to add flavour and crunch. They are especially good when marinated or added to stir-fry dishes. The thin red skins should be removed before use. To do this, simply immerse the nuts in a pan of boiling water for about 2 minutes, then drain and leave to cool; the skins will come off easily.

Prawns

For most of the recipes in this book you will need medium-to-large raw, unshelled prawns. These are sweeter and more succulent than ready-cooked ones. Before cooking, they should be shelled and, if large, de-veined. To remove the shell, twist off the head and discard, then, using your fingers, break open the shell along the belly and peel it off. Run a small, sharp knife along the back of the prawn and pull out the dark intestinal vein. The tail shell can be left on for presentation.

Rice

There are many different varieties of rice in China but long grain is the most popular. Although the Chinese go through the ritual of washing it, rice purchased at supermarkets doesn't require this step. However, if you wish to do as the Chinese do, put the rice into a large bowl, fill it with cold water and swish the rice around with your hands. Carefully pour off the cloudy water, keeping the rice in the bowl. Repeat this process several times until the water is clear.

Tiger prawns

Clockwise from top: chilli bean sauce, hoisin
sauce, yellow bean sauce, oyster sauce, chilli oil

Salt

Table salt is the finest grind but many cooks
believe that the coarser sea salt has a richer
flavour. Sea salt is frequently found in bins at
Chinese markets. Rock salt is often used in certain kinds of *chaozhou* (a cooking style from
southern China), especially with chicken dishes.

Salted Black Beans

These small black soya beans are fermented
with salt and spices to preserve them. Their
distinctive flavour makes them a tasty seasoning, especially when used with garlic or fresh
ginger. They are inexpensive and can be
obtained from Chinese grocers, usually in tins
labelled 'black beans in salted sauce', but you
may also see them packed in plastic bags. You
can rinse them before use as an optional step;
I prefer to chop them slightly, too, as this
helps to release their pungent flavour. Transfer
any unused beans and liquid to a sealed jar
and they will keep indefinitely in the refrigerator. For convenience, black bean sauce is now
available in supermarkets, which in many
cases is authentic and quite acceptable.

Sauces and Pastes

Chinese and Asian cookery involves a number
of tasty sauces and pastes. They are essential
for authentic Chinese cooking, and it is well
worth making the effort to obtain them. Most
are sold in bottles or tins by Chinese grocers
and some supermarkets. Once opened, tinned
sauces should be transferred to screw-top
glass jars and kept in the refrigerator, where
they will last indefinitely.

Chilli Bean Sauce

This thick, dark sauce or paste is made from
soya beans, chillies and other seasonings, and
is very hot and spicy. Be sure to seal the jar
tightly after use and store in the larder or
refrigerator. Do not confuse it with chilli sauce
(see below), which is a hotter, redder, thinner
condiment made without beans.

Chilli Sauce

This hot, bright-red sauce, made from chillies,
vinegar, sugar and salt, is mainly used as a
dipping sauce. There are various brands available in Chinese grocers and many supermarkets and you should experiment with them
until you find the one you like best. If you find
chilli sauce too strong, dilute it with hot water.
Do not confuse this sauce with chilli bean
sauce (see above), which is a much thicker,
darker sauce used for cooking.

Hoisin Sauce

This thick, dark, brownish-red sauce, made
from soya beans, vinegar, sugar, spices and
other flavourings, is sweet and spicy. It is sold
in tins and jars (it is sometimes also called
barbecue sauce) and is available in Chinese
grocers and supermarkets. If refrigerated, it
should keep indefinitely.

Oyster Sauce

This thick, brown sauce is made from a concentrate of oysters cooked in soy sauce and
brine. Despite its name, it does not taste fishy.
It has a rich flavour and is used not only in
cooking but also as a condiment, diluted with
a little oil, for vegetables, poultry and meat. It
is usually sold in bottles and can be bought in
Chinese grocers and supermarkets. I find it
keeps best in the refrigerator. A vegetarian
oyster sauce made with mushrooms is now
available.

Sesame Paste

This rich, thick, creamy brown paste is made from sesame seeds and is used in both hot and cold dishes. If you cannot obtain it, use peanut butter, which has a similar texture. Don't substitute tahini, the Middle Eastern sesame seed paste, since the flavour is not as strong.

Soy Sauce

Soy sauce is an essential ingredient in Chinese cooking. It is made from a mixture of soya beans, flour and water, which is then fermented naturally and aged for some months. The liquid that is finally distilled is soy sauce.

There are two main types. Light soy sauce, as the name implies, is light in colour, but it is full of flavour and is the better one to use for cooking. It is saltier than dark soy sauce, and is known in Chinese grocers as Superior Soy. Dark soy sauce, confusingly, is known as Soy Superior Sauce. It is aged for much longer than light soy sauce, hence its darker, almost black colour, and is also slightly thicker and stronger. It is more suitable for stews. I prefer it to light soy as a dipping sauce.

Supermarkets tend to sell dark soy sauce. Chinese grocers sell both types and the quality is excellent. Be sure you buy the correct one, as the names are very similar.

Whole Yellow Bean Sauce

This thick, spicy, aromatic sauce is made of yellow beans, flour and salt, which are fermented together. It is quite salty, and adds a distinctive flavour to Chinese sauces. There are two forms: whole beans in a thick sauce, and mashed or puréed beans (sold as crushed yellow bean sauce). I prefer the whole bean variety because it is slightly less salty and has a better texture.

Sesame Seeds

These are the dried seeds of the sesame herb. Unhulled, the seeds range from greyish white to black in colour. The tiny hulled seeds are cream coloured and pointed at one end. Stored in a glass jar in a cool, dry place, they will last indefinitely.

To toast sesame seeds, heat a frying pan, then add the seeds and stir occasionally. Watch them closely to make sure they don't burn. When they begin to brown lightly, after about 3–5 minutes, stir them again and tip them on to a plate. Leave to cool, then store in a glass jar in a cool, dark place.

Alternatively, you could spread the sesame seeds on a baking sheet and roast them in an oven preheated to 160°C/325°F/Gas Mark 3 for 10–15 minutes, until lightly browned.

Shaoxing Rice Wine

Rice wine is used extensively for cooking and drinking throughout China, but I believe the finest of its many varieties to be from Shaoxing in Zhejiang Province in eastern China. It is made from glutinous rice, yeast and spring water. Now readily available in Chinese markets and in some wine shops in the West, it should be kept tightly corked at room temperature. A good-quality, pale dry sherry can be substituted but cannot match its rich, mellow taste. Do not confuse this wine with sake, which is the Japanese version of rice wine and quite different. Western grape wines are not an adequate substitute either.

Sherry

If you cannot get rice wine, use a good-quality, dry pale sherry instead. Do not use sweet or cream sherries.

Sichuan Peppercorns

Sichuan peppercorns are known throughout China as 'flower peppers' because they look like flower buds opening. They are reddish brown, with a strong, pungent odour that distinguishes them from the hotter black peppercorns. They are actually not from peppers at all; instead they are the dried berries of a shrub belonging to the citrus family. Their smell reminds me of lavender but their taste is sharp and mildly spicy.

Sichuan peppercorns are inexpensive and will keep indefinitely if stored in a well-sealed container. They can be ground in a conventional peppermill and are very often roasted first to bring out the full flavour. To roast them, heat a wok or heavy frying-pan to a medium heat. Add the peppercorns (you can cook about 150 g (5 oz) at a time) and stir-fry them for about 5 minutes, until they brown slightly and start to smoke. Remove the pan from the heat and let them cool. Grind the peppercorns in a peppermill or a clean coffee grinder, or with a mortar and pestle. Store in a tightly

Spring onions (from top) finely chopped, shredded, cut on the round, cut on the diagonal sealed screw-top jar. Alternatively keep the whole roasted peppercorns in a well-sealed container and grind them when required.

Spinach

Western varieties of spinach are quite different from those used in China but they make satisfactory substitutes. Spinach is most commonly stir-fried, so frozen spinach is unsuitable since it is so moist. Chinese water spinach is the most common type in China and is available in Chinese markets in the West. It has hollow stems, delicate, pointed, green leaves, and a paler colour and milder flavour than common spinach. It should be cooked when very fresh, preferably on the day it is bought.

Spring Onions

The recipes in this book specify a variety of ways to prepare spring onions, both for cooking and for garnish. First, peel off the outer layer if it is bruised or damaged. Trim the tops and bottom and remove any damaged green tops.

To chop finely, split into quarters lengthways, then chop into small pieces horizontally. To shred, cut the onions in half horizontally, then split very finely lengthways. To curl shredded spring onions, put them in a bowl of ice-cold water. This makes an attractive garnish. Spring onions can also be cut simply on the round at various thicknesses, and also on the diagonal, which is useful for certain recipes and also looks pretty as a garnish.

Spring Roll Skins

These 15 cm (6 in) square, paper-thin wrappers are made from a soft flour and water dough. They are available in packets of 20 from Chinese grocers and keep well in the freezer if wrapped in clingfilm.

Star Anise

Star anise is a hard, star-shaped spice, the seed pod of an attractive bush. It is similar in flavour and fragrance to common anise but more robust and liquorice-like. Star anise is an essential ingredient in five-spice powder (see page 10) and is widely used in braised dishes, to which it imparts a rich taste and fragrance. It is available in plastic packs from Chinese grocers and should be stored in a sealed jar in a cool, dry place.

Sugar

Used sparingly, sugar helps to balance the flavours of sauces and other dishes. Chinese sugar comes in several forms: as rock or yellow lump sugar, as brown sugar slabs, and as maltose or malt sugar. I particularly like to use rock sugar, which has a richer, more subtle flavour than refined granulated sugar and gives a good lustre to braised dishes and sauces. It is available in packets from Chinese grocers. You may need to break the lumps into smaller pieces with a wooden mallet or rolling pin. If you cannot find it, use white sugar or coffee sugar crystals (the amber, chunky kind) instead.

Vinegar

Vinegars are widely used in Chinese cooking. Unlike Western vinegars, they are usually made from rice. There are many varieties, ranging in flavour from spicy and slightly tart to sweet and pungent. They can be bought in Chinese grocers and will keep indefinitely. If you cannot get Chinese vinegar, I suggest you use cider vinegar. Malt vinegar can be substituted if necessary but its taste is stronger and more acidic.

White Rice Vinegar

This clear vinegar has a mild flavour with a faint taste of glutinous rice. It is used in sweet and sour dishes.

Black Rice Vinegar

Black rice vinegar is very dark in colour and rich, though mild, in taste. It is used for braised dishes, sauces, and sometimes as a dipping sauce for crab.

Red Rice Vinegar

This is sweet and spicy, and is normally used as a dipping sauce for seafood.

Water Chestnuts

Water chestnuts are a white, sweet, crunchy bulb about the size of a walnut. In China they are often simmered in rock sugar and eaten as a snack. They are also used in cooked dishes, especially in southern China.

In the West, tinned water chestnuts are sold in many supermarkets and Chinese grocers. They have a good texture but little taste. Rinse them well in cold water before use and store

Clockwise from top: fresh water chestnuts,
star anise, Sichuan peppercorns, wonton skins

any unused ones in a jar of cold water. They
will keep for several weeks in the refrigerator
if you change the water daily. Fresh water
chestnuts can sometimes be obtained from
Chinese grocers or good supermarkets. They
are tastier than tinned ones and will keep,
unpeeled, in a paper bag in the refrigerator for
up to 2 weeks. Peel them before use and put
any leftover ones back in the refrigerator,
covered with cold water.

Wonton Skins

These thin, yellowish, pastry-like wrappings
made from egg and flour can be stuffed with
minced meat and fried, steamed or used in
soups. They are available fresh or frozen from
Chinese grocers or supermarkets, sold in little
piles of 8 cm (3¼ in) squares, wrapped in plastic. Fresh wonton skins will keep for about 5
days in the refrigerator if wrapped in clingfilm
or a plastic bag. If you are using frozen wonton skins, just peel off the number you require
and leave to thaw completely.

EQUIPMENT

Traditional cooking equipment is not essential for the preparation of Chinese food but in some cases will make it very much easier. These implements have been tested through many centuries of use. Once you become familiar with woks and clay pots, for example, you will have entered the culinary world of China.

Wok

All your faith in Chinese cookery and your own skills will come to nothing without a good wok. This versatile piece of equipment can be used not only for stir-frying but also for blanching, deep-frying and steaming. Its shape permits fuel-efficient, quick and even heating and cooking. When stir-frying, the deep sides prevent the food spilling over; when deep-frying, much less oil is required because of the tapered base of the wok.

There are two basic types: the traditional Cantonese version, with short, rounded handles on either side, and the *pau*, sometimes called the Peking wok, which has one 30–35 cm (12–14 in) long handle. The long-handled wok keeps you at a safer distance from the possibility of splashing hot oil or water.

The standard round-bottomed wok may only be used on gas hobs. Ones with flatter bottoms are now available, designed especially for electric hobs. Although this shape really defeats the purpose of the traditional design, which is to concentrate intense heat at the centre, it is better than an ordinary frying-pan because it has deeper sides.

Choosing a Wok

Choose a large wok – preferably about 30–35 cm (12–14 in) in diameter, with deep sides. It is easier and safer to cook a small batch of food in a large wok than a large quantity in a small one. Be aware that some modernized woks are too shallow or too flat-bottomed and thus no better than a frying-pan. A heavier wok, preferably made of carbon steel, is superior to the lighter stainless steel or aluminum type, which cannot take very high heat and tends to blacken, as well as scorch the food. Good non-stick carbon steel woks that maintain the heat without sticking are now on the market. They need special care to prevent scratching but in recent years the non-stick technology has improved, so that they can now be safely recommended. They are especially useful when cooking food that has a high acid level, such as lemons.

Seasoning a Wok

All woks except non-stick ones should be seasoned before first use. Many need to be scrubbed as well, to remove the machine oil that is applied to the surface by the manufacturer to protect it in transit. This is the only time you will ever need to scrub your wok – unless you let it become rusty.

Scrub it with a cream cleanser and water to remove as much of the machine oil as possible. Then dry it and put it on the hob on a low heat. Add 2 tablespoons of cooking oil and, using a wad of kitchen paper, rub the oil over the inside of the wok until the entire surface is lightly coated. Heat the wok slowly for about 10–15 minutes and then wipe it thoroughly with more kitchen paper. The paper will become blackened. Repeat this process of coating, heating and wiping until the kitchen paper comes clean. Your wok will darken and become well seasoned with use, which is a good sign.

Cleaning a Wok

Once your wok has been seasoned, you should never scrub it with soap or water. Just wash it in plain clear water and dry it thoroughly after each use – putting the cleaned wok over a low heat for a minute or two should do the trick. If it does rust a bit, scrub it with a cream cleanser and re-season it.

Stir-frying in a Wok

The most important thing when stir-frying is to have all your ingredients ready and to hand – this is a very fast method of cooking and you will not have time to stop and chop things while you are cooking.

Heat the wok until it is very hot, then add the oil and distribute it evenly over the surface using a metal spatula or long-handled spoon. It should be very hot – almost smoking – before you add the ingredients.

Add the food to be cooked and stir-fry by tossing it around the wok or pan with a metal spatula or long-handled spoon. If you are stir-frying meat, let each side rest for a few seconds before continuing to stir. Keep moving the food from the centre of the wok to the sides.

I prefer to use a long-handled wok, as there can be a lot of splattering due to the high temperature at which the food must be cooked.

Wok Accessories
Wok Stand
This is a metal ring or frame designed to keep a conventionally shaped wok steady on the hob. It is essential if you want to use your wok for steaming, deep-frying or braising. Stands come in two designs: a solid metal ring punched with about six ventilation holes, and a circular thin wire frame. If you have a gas cooker use only the latter type, as the more solid design does not allow for sufficient ventilation and may lead to a build-up of gas, which could put the flame out completely.

Wok Lid
This light, inexpensive domed cover, usually made from aluminium, is used for steaming. It is normally supplied with the wok but, if not, may be purchased at a Chinese or Asian market, or you may use any domed saucepan lid that fits snugly.

Spatula
A long-handled metal spatula shaped rather like a small shovel is ideal for scooping and tossing food in a wok. Alternatively any good long-handled spoon can be used.

Rack
When steaming food in your wok, you will need a wooden or metal rack or trivet to raise the food above the water level. Wok sets usually include a rack but, if not, Asian and Chinese grocers sell them separately. Department stores and hardware shops also sell wooden and metal stands which can serve the same purpose. Any rack, improvised or not, that keeps the food above the water so that it is steamed and not boiled will suffice.

Bamboo Brush
This bundle of stiff, split bamboo is used for cleaning a wok without scrubbing off the seasoned surface. It is an attractive, inexpensive implement but not essential. A soft washing-up brush will do just as well.

Chopping Board
One decided improvement over traditional Chinese cooking implements is the modern chopping board made of hardwood or white acrylic. Typical Chinese chopping boards are made of soft wood, which is difficult to maintain and, being soft, provides a fertile surface for bacteria. Hardwood or white acrylic boards are easy to clean, resist bacterial accumulation, and last much longer. Chinese cookery entails much chopping, slicing and dicing so it is essential to have a large, steady chopping board. For reasons of hygiene, never place cooked meat on a board on which raw meat or poultry has been prepared. For raw meat, always use a separate board and clean it thoroughly after each use.

Chopsticks
Many Western diners feel challenged by chopsticks, but I always encourage their use. Attempting any new technique is an interesting experience, and chopsticks do indeed offer the novice a physical entrée into Chinese cuisine. They are used as a combination spoon and fork, and for stirring, beating, whipping and mixing. But, of course, you can also get along nicely with Western spoons, forks, ladles, spatulas and whisks.

Chopsticks are cheap and readily available. I prefer the wooden ones but in China plastic ones are more commonly used (and reused) for hygienic and economic reasons.

Cleaver
To Chinese cooks, the cleaver is an all-purpose cutting instrument that makes all other knives redundant. Once you acquire some skill with a cleaver you will see how it can be used on all types of food to slice, dice, chop, fillet, shred, crush or whatever. In practice, most Chinese chefs rely upon three different sizes of cleaver – light, medium and heavy – to be used appropriately. Of course, you may use your own familiar kitchen knives instead, but if you decide to invest in a cleaver choose a good-quality stainless steel model and keep it sharpened.

Deep-fat Fryer
A deep-fat fryer is very useful and you may find it safer and easier to use for deep-frying than a wok. The quantities of oil given in the

Wok with lid, spatula, chopsticks, wok stand, cleaver and rack recipes in this book are based on the amount required for deep-frying in a wok. If you are using a deep-fat fryer instead, you will need about double that amount, but never fill it more than half-full with oil.

Rice Cooker

Electric rice cookers are increasing in popularity. They cook rice perfectly and keep it warm throughout the meal. They also have the advantage of freeing a burner or element so the hob is less cluttered. They are relatively expensive, however, so are only worth buying if you eat rice frequently.

Sand or Clay Pots

The Chinese rely upon these lightweight clay pots for braised dishes, soups and rice cooking. Their unglazed exteriors have a sandy texture, hence their name, and their design allows the infusion of aromas and tastes into foods. Clay pots are available in many sizes, with matching lids, and, being quite fragile, they are often encased in a wire frame. They should be used directly on the hob (most

Chinese do not have ovens) but never put an empty clay pot on a heated element or a hot one on a cold surface: the shock will crack it. Clay pots should always have at least some liquid in them and, when filled with food, they can take very high heat. If you have an electric cooker, use an asbestos pad to insulate the pot from direct contact with the hot coils. Note that because of the release of hot steam you should always lift the lid away from you.

Steamer

Steaming is not a very popular cooking method in the West. This is unfortunate because it is the best way of preparing many foods with a delicate taste and texture, such as fish and vegetables. In China, bamboo steamers have been in use for thousands of years. They come in several sizes of which the 25 cm (10 in) one is the most suitable for home use. The food is placed in the steamer, which is then placed above boiling water in a wok or pot. To stop the food sticking to the steamer as it cooks, put it on a layer of clean, damp muslin. A tight-fitting bamboo lid prevents the steam escaping; several steamers, stacked one above the other, may be used simultaneously.

Before using a bamboo steamer for the first time, wash it and then steam it with nothing in it for about 5 minutes. Of course, any kind of wide metal steamer may be used instead if you prefer.

Miscellaneous

Stainless steel bowls of different sizes, along with sieves and colanders, round out the list of basic implements. They are very useful because you will often have to drain or strain oils and juices and because you will be doing much mixing of wonderful foods. It is better to have one too many tools than one too few.

Clay pots and bamboo steamers

Conversion tables

Conversions are approximate and have been rounded up or down. Follow one set of measurements only – do not mix metric and Imperial.

Weights		Volume		Measurements	
Metric	**Imperial**	**Metric**	**Imperial**	**Metric**	**Imperial**
15 g	½ oz	25 ml	1 fl oz	0.5 cm	¼ inch
25 g	1 oz	50 ml	2 fl oz	1 cm	½ inch
40 g	1½ oz	85 ml	3 fl oz	2.5 cm	1 inch
50 g	2 oz	150 ml	5 fl oz (¼ pint)	5 cm	2 inches
75 g	3 oz	300 ml	10 fl oz (½ pint)	7.5 cm	3 inches
100 g	4 oz	450 ml	15 fl oz (¾ pint)	10 cm	4 inches
150 g	5 oz	600 ml	1 pint	15 cm	6 inches
175 g	6 oz	700 ml	1¼ pints	18 cm	7 inches
200 g	7 oz	900 ml	1½ pints	20 cm	8 inches
225 g	8 oz	1 litres	1¾ pints	23 cm	9 inches
250 g	9 oz	1.2 litres	2 pints	25 cm	10 inches
275 g	10 oz	1.25 litres	2¼ pints	30 cm	12 inches
350 g	12 oz	1.5 litres	2½ pints		
375 g	13 oz	1.6 litres	2¾ pints		

Oven temperatures		
140°C	275°F	Gas Mk 1
150°C	300°F	Gas Mk 2
160°C	325°F	Gas Mk 3
180°C	350°F	Gas Mk 4
190°C	375°F	Gas Mk 5
200°C	400°F	Gas Mk 6
220°C	425°F	Gas Mk 7
230°C	450°F	Gas Mk 8
240°C	475°F	Gas Mk 9

Weights		Volume	
400 g	14 oz	1.75 litres	3 pints
425 g	15 oz	1.8 litres	3¼ pints
450 g	1 lb	2 litres	3½ pints
550 g	1¼ lb	2.1 litres	3¾ pints
675 g	1½ lb	2.25 litres	4 pints
900 g	2 lb	2.75 litres	5 pints
1.5 kg	3 lb	3.4 litres	6 pints
1.75 kg	4 lb	3.9 litres	7 pints
2.25 kg	5 lb	5 litres	8 pints (1 gal)

SOUPS and STARTERS

Classic Chinese chicken stock

Your first step on the path to success with Chinese cooking is to prepare and maintain an ample supply of good chicken stock. I prefer to make a large amount and freeze it. Once you have a supply of stock available you will be able to prepare any number of soups or sauces very quickly.

makes about 3.4 litres (6 pints)
preparation time: 15 minutes
cooking time: 3–5 hours

Chicken stock is light, delicious and inexpensive to make. It marries well with other foods, enhancing and sustaining them. Small wonder that it is an almost universally present ingredient in Chinese cookery, from the Imperial kitchens to the most humble food stalls. The usual Chinese chicken stock is very simple: the essence of chicken, often with complements of ginger and spring onion added. Combined with the condiments that give Chinese food its distinctive flavour, good stock captures the essential taste of China. The simple recipe given here reflects what I believe works best for any Chinese dish. The classic Chinese method of ensuring a clear stock is to blanch the meat and bones before simmering. I find this unnecessary. My method of careful skimming achieves the same result with far less work.

Commercially prepared tinned or dried stocks are available but many of them are of inferior quality, since they are either too salty or contain additives and colourings that can adversely affect your health as well as the natural taste of good food. Stock does take time to prepare but it is easy to make your own – and home-made is the best. Here are several important points to keep in mind when making stock:

- Good stock requires meat to give it richness and flavour. It is therefore essential to use at least some chicken meat, if not a whole bird.
- Use a tall, heavy pot so the liquid covers all the solids and evaporation is slow.
- The stock should never boil. If it does it will become cloudy and the fat will be incorporated into the liquid. Flavour and digestibility come with a clear stock.
- Simmer the stock slowly and skim it regularly. Be patient; you will reap the rewards each time you prepare a Chinese dish.
- Strain the finished stock well through several layers of muslin or a fine sieve.
- Allow the stock to cool thoroughly, then chill and remove any fat before freezing it.

2 kg (4½ lb) raw chicken feet, wings, etc, or any leftover bones you may have (save uncooked chicken bones and keep them in the freezer until you need them)

675 g (1½ lb) chicken pieces, such as wings, thighs, drumsticks

5 litres (8 pints) cold water

3 slices of fresh root ginger, cut into diagonal slices 5 x 1 cm (2 x ½ in)

6 spring onions, green tops removed

6 garlic cloves, unpeeled but lightly crushed

1 teaspoon salt

1 Put all the chicken into a very large pot (the bones can be put in either frozen or defrosted). Cover with the cold water and bring to a simmer.

2 Using a large, shallow spoon, skim off the scum as it rises to the surface of the water from the bones. Watch the heat, as the stock should never boil. Keep skimming as necessary until the stock looks clear. This can take 20–40 minutes at a low simmer. Do not stir or disturb the stock.

3 Now add the ginger, spring onions, garlic cloves and salt. Simmer the stock on a very low heat for 2–4 hours, skimming any fat off the top at least twice. The stock should be rich and full-bodied, which is why it needs to be simmered for such a long time.

4 Strain the stock through several layers of dampened muslin or through a very fine sieve. Let it cool thoroughly, then chill. Remove any fat that has risen to the top. It is now ready to be used or transferred to containers and frozen for future use.

Cantonese egg flower soup

This easy soup is found in almost every Chinese restaurant. No wonder; it is tasty and fantastically exotic. Lightly beaten egg lies flat on the surface of the soup like lilies on a pond. This effect is created by gently guiding the egg over the soup in strands instead of dropping the mixture in all at once, which would cause it to lump together. The egg mixture slightly thickens the soup, which nonetheless remains very light. As with any good soup, the most important thing is the stock upon which it is based.

1 egg, lightly beaten

2 teaspoons sesame oil

1.2 litres (2 pints) *Classic Chinese chicken stock* (see page 26) or good-quality bought stock

1 teaspoon sugar

1 teaspoon salt

1 tablespoon light soy sauce

3 tablespoons finely shredded spring onions, white part only

3 tablespoons finely shredded green spring onion tops, to garnish

serves 4
preparation time: 5 minutes
cooking time: 5 minutes

1 Put the egg and sesame oil in a small jug or bowl, mix with a fork and set aside.

2 Put the stock into a pot and bring to a simmer. Add the sugar, salt and soy sauce and stir to mix them in well. Stir in the white part of the spring onions.

3 Next add the egg mixture in a very slow, thin stream.

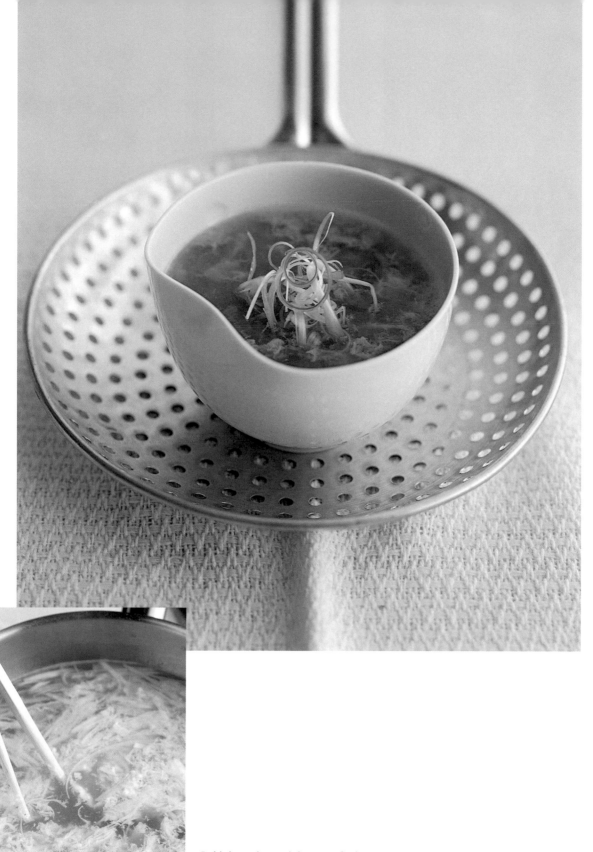

4 Using chopsticks or a fork, pull the egg slowly into strands. I find that stirring the egg in a figure of eight works quite well. Garnish with the green spring onion tops.

Sweetcorn and crab soup

This popular Chinese soup has captivated Western diners. My mother often made it using fresh sweetcorn. For convenience, tinned or frozen corn may be substituted but I think my mother's recipe is superior.

serves 4
preparation time: 5 minutes
cooking time: 10 minutes

450 g (1 lb) corn on the cob, or 275 g (10 oz) tinned or frozen sweetcorn

1 egg white

1 teaspoon sesame oil

1.2 litres (2 pints) *Classic Chinese chicken stock* (see page 26) or good-quality bought stock

1 tablespoon Shaoxing rice wine or dry sherry

1 tablespoon light soy sauce

2 teaspoons finely chopped fresh root ginger

1 teaspoon salt

½ teaspoon freshly ground white pepper

1 teaspoon sugar

2 teaspoons cornflour, blended with 2 teaspoons water

225 g (8 oz) fresh or frozen crabmeat

2 tablespoons finely chopped spring onions, to garnish

1 If you are using fresh corn, pull back the husks, wash the cobs and then remove the kernels with a sharp knife or cleaver. You should end up with about 275 g (10 oz) corn.

2 Mix the egg white and sesame oil together in a small jug or bowl and set aside.

3 Bring the stock to the boil in a large pot and add the corn. Simmer for 5 minutes, uncovered, then add the rice wine or sherry, light soy sauce, ginger, salt, pepper, sugar and the cornflour mixture. Bring back to the boil, then lower the heat to a simmer. Add the crabmeat.

4 Immediately afterwards, slowly pour in the egg white mixture in a steady stream, stirring all the time. Transfer the soup to a tureen or individual bowls and garnish with the spring onions.

Cantonese wonton soup

This is one of the most popular soups in food stalls throughout southern China and it is equally popular in Chinese restaurants in the West. Soup wonton should be stuffed savoury dumplings poached in clear water and then served in a rich broth. Unfortunately in many restaurants the soup arrives with wonton skins but very little filling. This recipe will enable you to make a simple but authentic wonton soup. Wonton skins can be obtained, fresh or frozen, from Chinese grocers.

225 g (8 oz) wonton skins, thawed if necessary

1.2 litres (2 pints) *Classic Chinese chicken stock* (see page 26) or good-quality bought stock

1 tablespoon light soy sauce

1 teaspoon sesame oil

Chopped green spring onion tops, to garnish

For the filling:

225 g (8 oz) raw prawns, peeled, de-veined (see page 13) and coarsely chopped

225 g (8 oz) minced fatty pork

1 teaspoon salt

½ teaspoon freshly ground black pepper

1½ tablespoons light soy sauce

3 tablespoons finely chopped spring onions (white part only)

2 teaspoons finely chopped fresh root ginger

1 tablespoon Shaoxing rice wine or dry sherry

1 teaspoon sugar

2 teaspoons sesame oil

1 egg white, lightly beaten

serves 4

preparation time: 30 minutes, plus at least 20 minutes' chilling

cooking time: 10 minutes

1 For the filling, put the prawns and pork in a large bowl, add the salt and pepper and mix well, either by kneading with your hand or stirring with a wooden spoon.

2 Add all the other filling ingredients and mix thoroughly. Cover the bowl with clingfilm and chill for at least 20 minutes.

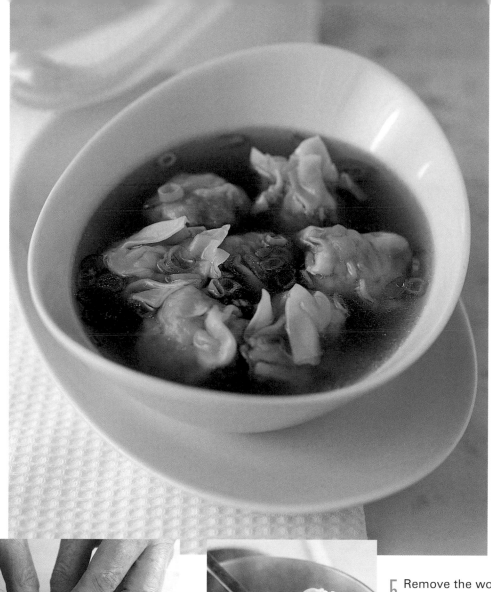

5 Remove the wontons immediately and transfer them to
the pot of stock. (Poaching
them first results in a cleaner-
tasting broth.) Simmer them
in the stock for 2 minutes.
Transfer to a soup tureen or
individual bowls, garnish
with the spring onion tops
and serve immediately.

3 To stuff the wontons, put
1 tablespoon of the filling in
the centre of each wonton
skin. Dampen the edges with
a little water and bring them
up around the filling. Pinch
the edges together at the top
so that the wonton is sealed;
it should look like a small,
filled bag.

4 Put the stock, soy sauce and
sesame oil in a large pot and
bring to a simmer. Mean-
while, bring a large pan of
salted water to the boil and
poach the wontons in it, in
batches, for 1 minute or until
they float to the top.

Spicy hot and sour soup

This northern and western Chinese soup has become quite popular in the Western world because it is a hearty dish, suited to cold climates. It combines sour and spicy elements in a rich, tasty stock and reheats very well. The list of ingredients may look daunting but in fact the soup is quite easy to make. Replete with contrasting textures and flavours, it makes an engaging alternative to Western-style soups.

1.2 litres (2 pints) *Classic Chinese chicken stock* (see page 26) or good-quality bought stock

2 teaspoons salt

100 g (4 oz) lean pork, finely shredded

25 g (1 oz) Chinese dried mushrooms, soaked, stems removed (see page 11)

15 g (½ oz) dried tree fungus or wood ear fungus, soaked, stems removed (see page 11)

225 g (8 oz) fresh firm beancurd, drained

2 eggs, beaten with a pinch of salt

4 teaspoons sesame oil

1½ tablespoons light soy sauce

1 tablespoon dark soy sauce

1 teaspoon freshly ground white pepper

6 tablespoons Chinese white rice vinegar or cider vinegar

2 teaspoons chilli oil

2 tablespoons finely chopped fresh coriander

For the marinade:

1 teaspoon light soy sauce

1 teaspoon Shaoxing rice wine or dry sherry

½ teaspoon sesame oil

½ teaspoon cornflour

A pinch of salt

A pinch of sugar

serves 4
preparation time: 25 minutes
cooking time: 5 minutes

1 Bring the stock to a simmer in a large pot and add the salt. Meanwhile, combine the pork with the marinade ingredients, mix well and set aside.

2 Finely shred the soaked mushrooms, tree or wood ear fungus and beancurd and set aside. In a small bowl, combine the eggs with 2 teaspoons of the sesame oil.

5 Remove the soup from the heat, and add the soy sauces, white pepper and vinegar. Give the soup a good stir, then stir in the remaining sesame oil, plus the chilli oil and coriander. Ladle into a soup tureen or individual bowls and serve.

3 Stir the pork into the stock and simmer for 1 minute. Then add the mushrooms and beancurd and simmer for a further 2 minutes.

4 Pour in the egg mixture in a slow, thin, steady stream. Using chopsticks or a fork, pull the egg slowly into strands.

Crispy 'seaweed'

This is one of the most popular Chinese restaurant dishes in the West. A special type of seaweed is used in China but it is not yet available elsewhere so Chinese cabbage is used instead. This is a good example of the adaptability of Chinese cuisine: if the original ingredients are not available, technique and ingenuity will overcome the deficiency. This dish is delicious and easy to make, and, speaking of adaptability, can also be tried with fresh spinach leaves.

serves 4
preparation time: 20 minutes
cooking time: 20 minutes

1.25 kg (2½ lb) bok choy
    (Chinese white cabbage)
900 ml (1½ pints) groundnut
    oil

1 teaspoon salt
2 teaspoons sugar
50 g (2 oz) pine kernels,
    lightly roasted

1 Separate the stalks from the stem of the bok choy and then cut the green leaves from the white stalks. (Save the stalks; you can stir-fry them with garlic – see *Stir-fried broccoli* on page 98 – or use them for soup.)

2 Wash the leaves in several changes of cold water, then drain them thoroughly and dry in a salad spinner. Roll the leaves up tightly, a few at a time, and finely shred them into strips 5 mm (¼ in) wide.

3 Spread them out on a baking sheet and put them in an oven preheated to 120°C/250°F/Gas Mark ½ for 15 minutes to dry slightly. They should not be completely dry or they will burn when fried. Remove from the oven and leave to cool. This can be done the day before.

5 Toss the crispy greens with the salt and sugar. Garnish with the pine kernels and serve.

4 Heat a wok over a high heat, then add the oil. When the oil is hot and slightly smoking, deep-fry the greens in 3 or 4 batches. After about 30–40 seconds, when they turn crisp and green, remove them immediately from the wok and drain well on kitchen paper. Leave to cool.

Sesame prawn toast

Sesame prawn toast is often served as an appetizer in Chinese restaurants. Its origins are rather obscure but I suspect it is a variation on the prawn paste used widely in southern China as a stuffing or for deep-frying into crispy balls.

makes about 30 pieces
preparation time: 25 minutes
cooking time: 25 minutes

10 thin slices of white bread

3 tablespoons white sesame seeds

450 ml (15 fl oz) groundnut oil

For the prawn paste:

450 g (1 lb) raw prawns, shelled and de-veined (see page 13)

100 g (4 oz) fresh or tinned water chestnuts, peeled if fresh, finely chopped

100 g (4 oz) minced fatty pork

1 teaspoon salt

½ teaspoon freshly ground black pepper

1 egg white

3 tablespoons finely chopped spring onions (white part only)

1½ tablespoons finely chopped fresh root ginger

1 tablespoon light soy sauce

2 teaspoons sesame oil

2 teaspoons sugar

1 Using a cleaver or sharp knife, chop the prawns coarsely and then mince them finely into a paste. Put them into a bowl and mix in the rest of the ingredients for the prawn paste. (Alternatively, you could do all this in a food processor.) The paste can be made several hours in advance and kept, covered, in the refrigerator.

2 Remove the crusts from the bread and cut it into rectangles about 7.5 x 2.5 cm (3 x 1 in) – you should have about 3 pieces per slice. If the bread is fresh, place it in a warm oven to dry out a little. Dry bread will absorb less oil.

3 Spread the prawn paste thickly on each piece of bread. The paste should form a mound about 3 mm (⅛ in) deep, although you can spread it more thinly if you prefer. Sprinkle the toasts with the sesame seeds.

4 Heat the oil to a moderate heat in a wok or deep-fat fryer. Deep-fry several prawn toasts at a time, paste-side down, for 2–3 minutes. Then turn them over and deep-fry for another 2 minutes, until they are golden brown.

5 Remove with a slotted spoon, drain on kitchen paper and serve.

Crispy fried wontons

Another favourite with Chinese-food lovers. Ordinary wontons become savoury treats when dipped in a sweet and sour sauce. They make a great snack or starter for any meal. The sweet and sour sauce can be made a day in advance, refrigerated, and then brought to room temperature before serving. The recipe can easily be doubled for those who want more sauce. Wonton skins can be bought fresh or frozen from Chinese grocers.

225 g (8 oz) wonton skins, thawed if necessary

600 ml (1 pint) groundnut or vegetable oil

For the filling:

350 g (12 oz) raw prawns, shelled, de-veined (see page 13) and coarsely minced or chopped

100 g (4 oz) minced fatty pork

2 teaspoons salt

½ teaspoon freshly ground black pepper

4 tablespoons finely chopped spring onions

2 teaspoons finely chopped fresh root ginger

2 teaspoons Shaoxing rice wine or dry sherry

1 teaspoon sugar

2 teaspoons sesame oil

1 egg white, lightly beaten

For the sweet and sour dipping sauce:

150 ml (5 fl oz) water

2 tablespoons sugar

3 tablespoons Chinese white rice vinegar or cider vinegar

3 tablespoons tomato paste or tomato ketchup

1 teaspoon salt

¼ teaspoon freshly ground white pepper

1 teaspoon cornflour, blended with 2 teaspoons water

serves 6
preparation time: 35 minutes, plus at least 20 minutes' chilling
cooking time: 20 minutes

1 For the filling, put the prawns and pork in a bowl, add the salt and pepper and mix well, either by kneading with your hand or stirring with a wooden spoon. Add all the remaining filling ingredients and stir well. Cover with clingfilm and chill for at least 20 minutes.

2 In a small saucepan, combine all the ingredients for the sweet and sour sauce except the cornflour mixture. Bring to the boil, stir in the cornflour mixture and cook for 1 minute. Remove from the heat and leave to cool.

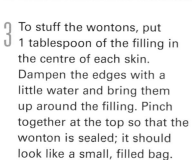

5 Drain the wontons well on kitchen paper, then serve immediately with the sweet and sour sauce.

3 To stuff the wontons, put 1 tablespoon of the filling in the centre of each skin. Dampen the edges with a little water and bring them up around the filling. Pinch together at the top so that the wonton is sealed; it should look like a small, filled bag.

4 Heat a wok over a high heat. Add the oil and, when it is very hot and slightly smoking, deep-fry the wontons, a handful at a time, for 2–3 minutes or until golden and crisp. If they brown too quickly, reduce the heat slightly.

Dim sum-style pork dumplings

Chinese restaurant diners usually enjoy discovering these tea-house treats, which have always been a favourite of the southern Chinese. They are simply stuffed wontons (egg dough dumplings) that have been steamed instead of poached or deep-fried. Steaming gives them a more pronounced, yet subtle, taste and texture. Wonton skins can be obtained fresh or frozen from Chinese grocers.

1 packet of wonton skins
  (about 40), thawed if
  necessary
A little vegetable oil

makes about 40
preparation time: 30 minutes
cooking time: 20 minutes
  per batch

For the filling:

100 g (4 oz) fresh or tinned
  water chestnuts, peeled if
  fresh, finely chopped

100 g (4 oz) raw prawns,
  shelled, de-veined (see
  page 13) and coarsely
  chopped

350 g (12 oz) minced fatty pork

2 tablespoons finely chopped
  Parma ham or lean smoked
  bacon

1 tablespoon light soy sauce

1 teaspoon dark soy sauce

1 tablespoon Shaoxing rice
  wine or dry sherry

3 tablespoons finely chopped
  spring onions

2 teaspoons finely chopped
  fresh root ginger

2 teaspoons sesame oil

1 egg white, lightly beaten

1 teaspoon salt

½ teaspoon freshly ground
  black pepper

2 teaspoons sugar

1 To make the filling, put all the ingredients in a bowl and mix together thoroughly.

2 Place a portion of the filling on each wonton skin. Bring up the sides and press them around the filling mixture. Tap the dumpling on the bottom to make a flat base. The top should be wide open, exposing the filling.

3 Set up a steamer or put a rack inside a wok or large, deep pot. Pour in about 5 cm (2 in) of water and bring to the boil. Oil the rack, or the inside of the steamer to prevent the dumplings sticking. Put the dumplings on it (you may have to cook them in several batches).

4 Cover the pot tightly, turn the heat to low and steam gently for about 20 minutes. To save time, use a larger steamer to cook bigger batches. Serve the dumplings hot; they can be reheated if necessary by steaming gently for a few minutes.

Peking-style caramel walnuts

This Peking-style dish is increasing in popularity throughout the West as more non-Cantonese recipes make their way on to Chinese restaurant menus. The shelled walnuts must be blanched first to rid them of any bitterness. Then they are rolled in sugar, left to dry for several hours and deep-fried to caramelize the sugar coating. Finally they are rolled in sesame seeds. The result is a classic contrast of tastes and textures. They can be served hot or cold and are perfect with drinks.

225 g (8 oz) shelled walnuts
100 g (4 oz) granulated sugar
450 ml (15 fl oz) groundnut oil
3 tablespoons sesame seeds

serves 4
preparation time: 10 minutes,
    plus at least 2 hours' drying
cooking time: 15 minutes

1 Bring a large pan of water to the boil, add the walnuts and then simmer for about 5 minutes. Drain through a colander or sieve.

2 Pat the walnuts dry with kitchen paper and spread them on a baking tray. Sprinkle the sugar over the warm nuts and roll them in it to coat them completely. Place the tray in a cool, draughty place and leave to dry for at least 2 hours, preferably overnight. (They can be prepared ahead to this point.)

3 Heat the oil to a moderate heat in a wok or deep-fat fryer. Fry a batch of the walnuts for about 2 minutes or until the sugar melts and the walnuts turn golden (adjust the heat if necessary to prevent burning). Remove the nuts from the oil.

4 Sprinkle them with the sesame seeds and lay them on a wire rack to cool. (Do not drain them on kitchen paper or the sugar will stick when it dries.) Deep-fry and drain the rest of the walnuts in the same way. Serve warm or cold. Once cooled, the caramel walnuts can be kept in a sealed glass jar for about 2 weeks.

Spring rolls

Spring rolls are one of the best-known Chinese snacks. They are not difficult to make and are a perfect starter for any meal. They should be crisp, light and delicate. Spring roll skins can be obtained fresh or frozen from Chinese grocers.

1 packet of spring roll skins, thawed if necessary

1 egg, beaten

1.2 litres (2 pints) groundnut oil for deep-frying

1 quantity of *Sweet and sour dipping sauce* (see page 40)

For the filling:

100 g (4 oz) raw prawns, shelled, de-veined (see page 13) and minced or very finely chopped

100 g (4 oz) minced fatty pork

1½ tablespoons groundnut oil

2 tablespoons coarsely chopped garlic

1 tablespoon finely chopped fresh root ginger

1½ tablespoons light soy sauce

1 tablespoon Shaoxing rice wine or dry sherry

3 tablespoons finely chopped spring onions

1 teaspoon salt

½ teaspoon freshly ground black pepper

225 g (8 oz) Chinese leaves (Peking cabbage), finely shredded

25 g (1 oz) dried Chinese black mushrooms, soaked, stems removed (see page 11), and finely shredded

For the marinade:

1 teaspoon light soy sauce

1 teaspoon Shaoxing rice wine or dry sherry

1 teaspoon sesame oil

½ teaspoon salt

½ teaspoon freshly ground black pepper

makes about 15–18
preparation time: 40 minutes
cooking time: 20 minutes

1 For the filling, combine the prawns and pork with all the marinade ingredients in a small bowl.

2 Heat a wok over a high heat. Add the 1½ tablespoons of groundnut oil and, when it is very hot and slightly smoking, add the garlic and ginger and stir-fry for 20 seconds.

3 Add all the rest of the filling ingredients, including the prawn and meat mixture, and stir-fry for 5 minutes. Place the mixture in a colander to drain and allow it to cool thoroughly.

4 Place 3–4 tablespoons of the filling near the end of each spring roll skin, then fold in the sides and roll up tightly.

5 Left: Seal the open end by brushing a small amount of the beaten egg along the edge, then pressing together gently. You should have a roll about 10 cm (4 ins) long, a little like an oversized cigar.

6 Rinse out the wok and reheat it over a high heat, then add the oil for deep-frying. When the oil is hot and slightly smoking, gently drop in as many spring rolls as will fit easily in one layer.

7 Fry the spring rolls until golden brown and cooked through, about 4 minutes. Adjust the heat as necessary. Remove with a slotted spoon, drain on a wire rack then on kitchen paper. Cook the remaining spring rolls in the same way. Serve them at once, hot and crispy, with the sweet and sour sauce for dipping.

FISH and SHELLFISH

Steamed Cantonese-style fish

Steaming is a favourite Chinese cooking method for fish. A simple but gentle technique, it doesn't mask the fresh taste of the fish, which remains moist and tender, and you can savour the combination of the other ingredients. An added bonus is that it is very healthy. Always buy the freshest possible fish and ask your fishmonger to prepare it for cooking.

serves 4
preparation time: 10 minutes
cooking time: 5–15 minutes

450 g (1 lb) firm white fish fillets, such as cod or sole, skinned, or a whole fish such as sole or turbot

1 teaspoon coarse sea salt or plain salt

1½ tablespoons finely shredded fresh root ginger

3 tablespoons finely shredded spring onions

2 tablespoons light soy sauce

2 teaspoons dark soy sauce

1 tablespoon groundnut oil

2 teaspoons sesame oil

Fresh coriander sprigs, to garnish

1 Pat the fish dry with kitchen paper and evenly rub with the salt, rubbing it inside the cavity as well if you are using a whole fish. Put the fish on a heatproof plate and scatter the ginger evenly over the top.

2 Set up a steamer or put a rack into a wok or deep pan. Fill it with 5 cm (2 in) of water and bring to the boil over a high heat. Put the plate of fish on the rack, cover tightly and steam the fish until it is just cooked. Flat fish fillets will take about 5 minutes; whole fish, or fillets such as sea bass, will take 12–14 minutes. The fish should turn opaque and flake slightly but still remain moist.

3 Remove the plate of cooked fish and pour off any liquid that may have accumulated. Scatter the spring onions on the fish, then drizzle over the light and dark soy sauces.

4 Heat the two oils together in a small saucepan until smoking, then immediately pour them over the fish. Garnish with coriander and serve at once.

Sichuan braised fish

This quick and easy dish is bursting with the spicy flavours of Sichuan. A firm, white fish such as cod, sea bass, halibut or haddock is most suitable for braising.

serves 4
preparation time: 15 minutes
cooking time: 10 minutes

450 g (1 lb) fresh firm white fish fillets, such as cod, sea bass or halibut, skinned

1 teaspoon salt

Cornflour for dusting

150 ml (5 fl oz) groundnut oil

3 spring onions, cut into 5 cm (2 in) slices on the diagonal

1 tablespoon finely chopped garlic

2 teaspoons finely chopped fresh root ginger

For the sauce:

150 ml (5 fl oz) *Classic Chinese chicken stock* (see page 26) or good-quality bought stock

1 teaspoon whole yellow bean sauce

1 tablespoon chilli bean sauce

2 tablespoons Shaoxing rice wine or dry sherry

2 teaspoons dark soy sauce

2 teaspoons sugar

2 teaspoons sesame oil

½ teaspoon salt

¼ teaspoon freshly ground white pepper

1 Sprinkle the fish fillets evenly on both sides with the salt. Cut them into strips 5 x 2.5 cm (2 x 1 in) and leave for 20 minutes.

2 Dust the strips of fish liberally with cornflour.

3 Heat a wok over a high heat. Add the oil and, when it is very hot and slightly smoking, turn the heat down. Fry the pieces of fish on both sides until they are lightly browned. Remove from the wok and drain on kitchen paper.

4 Pour off most of the oil, leaving about a tablespoon in the wok. Re-heat the wok, then add the spring onions, garlic and ginger and stir-fry for 30 seconds.

5 Add all the sauce ingredients and bring to the boil. Turn the heat down to a simmer and return the fish to the pan. Simmer for about 2–3 minutes, then serve.

Sweet and sour prawns

Perhaps one of the most popular and best-known Chinese dishes in the West. It is simple to make, and the sweet, pungent flavours of the sauce combine well with the firm, succulent prawns.

serves 4
preparation time: 25 minutes
cooking time: 5 minutes

1½ tablespoons groundnut oil

1½ tablespoons coarsely chopped garlic

2 teaspoons finely chopped fresh root ginger

4 spring onions, cut into 4 cm (1½ in) pieces diagonally

450 g (1 lb) raw prawns, shelled and de-veined (see page 13)

100 g (4 oz) red or green pepper, cut into 2.5 cm (1 in) squares

225 g (8 oz) fresh or tinned water chestnuts, peeled if fresh, sliced

For the sauce:

150 ml (5 fl oz) *Classic Chinese chicken stock* (see page 26) or good-quality bought stock

2 tablespoons Shaoxing rice wine or dry sherry

3 tablespoons light soy sauce

2 teaspoons dark soy sauce

1½ tablespoons tomato paste

3 tablespoons Chinese white rice vinegar or cider vinegar

1 tablespoon sugar

1 tablespoon cornflour, blended with 2 tablespoons water

1 Heat a wok over a high heat, then add the oil. When it is very hot and slightly smoking, add the garlic, ginger and spring onions and stir-fry for 20 seconds.

2 Add the prawns and stir-fry them for 1 minute.

3 Next add the pepper and water chestnuts and stir-fry for 30 seconds.

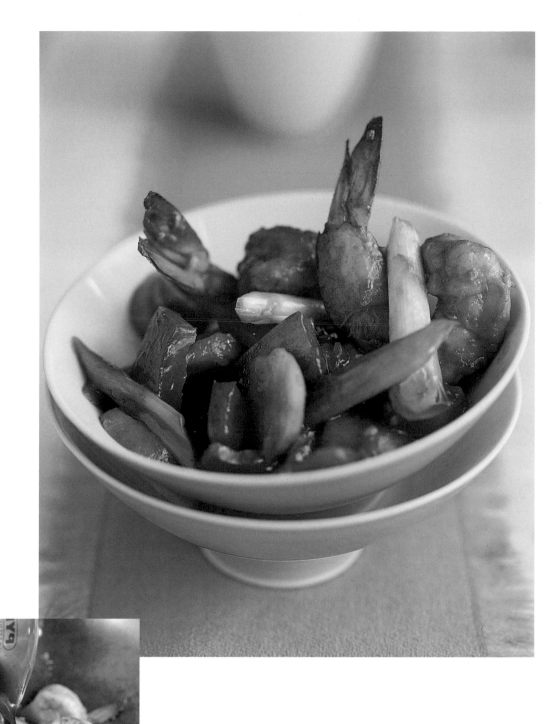

4 Now add all the sauce ingredients except the cornflour mixture. Bring to the boil, add the cornflour mixture, then turn the heat down and simmer for 3 minutes. Serve immediately.

Spicy Sichuan-style prawns

Sichuan cooking is popular throughout China and in recent years adventurous Chinese restaurant diners have discovered how delicious it can be. This is one of the best-known dishes from that area.

serves 4
preparation time: 25 minutes
cooking time: 5 minutes

1½ tablespoons groundnut oil

2 teaspoons finely chopped fresh root ginger

1 tablespoon coarsely chopped garlic

2 tablespoons finely chopped spring onions

450 g (1 lb) raw prawns, shelled and de-veined (see page 13)

For the sauce:

1 tablespoon tomato paste

2 teaspoons chilli bean sauce

2 teaspoons Chinese black vinegar or cider vinegar

½ teaspoon salt

½ teaspoon freshly ground black pepper

2 teaspoons sugar

2 teaspoons sesame oil

Fresh coriander sprigs, to garnish (optional)

1 Heat a wok over a high heat. Add the oil and, when it is very hot and slightly smoking, add the ginger, garlic and spring onions.

2 Stir-fry for 20 seconds, then add the prawns. Stir-fry the prawns for about 1 minute.

3 Add all the sauce ingredients and continue to stir-fry for another 3 minutes over a high heat. Serve at once.

Stir-fried squid with vegetables

Squid cooked the Chinese way is both tender and tasty. The secret is to blanch it in boiling water, then cook it for the minimum amount of time – just enough to firm it up slightly. Cooking it for too long will make it tough, so that eating it is like chewing on rubber bands. This recipe can also be prepared with prawns if you find squid difficult to obtain.

serves 4
preparation time: 25 minutes
cooking time: 10 minutes

450 g (1 lb) cleaned and prepared squid

1½ tablespoons groundnut oil

2 tablespoons coarsely chopped garlic

1 tablespoon finely chopped fresh root ginger

100 g (4 oz) red or green pepper, cut into thin strips

100 g (4 oz) mangetout, trimmed

3 tablespoons *Classic Chinese chicken stock* (see page 26) or good-quality bought stock

1 tablespoon Shaoxing rice wine or dry sherry

3 tablespoons oyster sauce

1 tablespoon light soy sauce

2 teaspoons dark soy sauce

2 teaspoons salt

2 teaspoons of cornflour, blended with 2 teaspoons water

2 teaspoons sesame oil

1 If the tentacles are still attached to the head of the squid, cut them off and reserve. Discard the head. Cut the squid bodies into 4-cm (1½-in) strips.

2 Blanch the strips and tentacles by simmering them in a large pan of boiling water for 15 seconds. The squid will firm up slightly and turn an opaque white colour. Remove and drain in a colander.

3 Heat a wok over a high heat, then add the oil. When it is very hot and slightly smoking, add the garlic and ginger and stir-fry for 15 seconds. Then add the pepper strips and mangetout and stir-fry for 1 minute.

4 Add all the rest of the ingredients except the squid and sesame oil and bring the mixture to the boil.

5 Give it a stir, then add the squid and mix well. Cook for 30 seconds more, stir in the sesame oil and serve at once.

STIR-FRIED SQUID WITH VEGETABLES | 61

Cantonese crab with black bean sauce

This recipe reflects the popularity of black beans, which go well with almost any food. It is a great favourite in many Chinese restaurants. However, it can only be made with fresh crabs in the shell, since the shell protects the delicate crabmeat during the stir-frying process. If you can't get crab in the shell, use prawns instead. I have added some minced pork – a Chinese trick which helps to stretch the expensive crabmeat. The Chinese traditionally eat the crab with their fingers. I suggest you have a large bowl of water decorated with lemon slices on the table so that your guests can rinse their fingers.

serves 4–6
preparation time: 20 minutes
cooking time: 20 minutes

1 live or freshly cooked crab in the shell, weighing about 1.5 kg (3 lb)

2 tablespoons groundnut oil

3 tablespoons coarsely chopped salted black beans

2 tablespoons coarsely chopped garlic

1 tablespoon finely chopped fresh root ginger

3 tablespoons finely chopped spring onions

225 g (8 oz) minced pork

2 tablespoons light soy sauce

1 tablespoon dark soy sauce

2 tablespoons Shaoxing rice wine or dry sherry

250 ml (8 fl oz) *Classic Chinese chicken stock* (see page 26) or good-quality bought stock

2 eggs, beaten

2 teaspoons sesame oil

1 To cook a live crab, bring a large pot of water to the boil, add 2 teaspoons of salt and then put in the crab. Cover the pot and cook the crab for about 5–7 minutes, until it turns bright red. Remove with a slotted spoon and drain in a colander. Leave to cool.

2 Place the cooked crab on its back on a board. Using your fingers, twist the claws from the body. They should come off quite easily.

3 Now twist off the bony tail flap on the underside of the crab and discard it. With your fingers, pry the body from the main shell. Remove and discard the small, bag-like stomach sac and its appendages, which are located just behind the crab's mouth.

4 Pull the soft, feathery gills, which look a little like fingers, away from the body and discard them. Remove the legs and put to one side.

5 Using a cleaver or heavy knife, split the crab shell in half and, using a spoon, fork or skewer, scrape out all the brown crabmeat.

6 Using a cleaver or heavy knife, cut the crab, shell included, into large pieces. Crack the claws and legs slightly.

7 Heat a wok over a high heat. Add the oil and, when it is very hot and slightly smoking, add the black beans, garlic, ginger and spring onions and stir-fry for 20 seconds.

8 Then add the pork and stir-fry for 1 minute. Add the crab pieces and all the remaining ingredients except the eggs and the sesame oil. Stir-fry over a high heat for about 10 minutes.

9 Combine the eggs with the sesame oil and then gradually pour this into the crab mixture, stirring slowly. There should be light strands of egg trailing over the crab mixture. Turn it on to a large, warm platter, or arrange in crab claws and serve.

Steamed fresh oysters

Steaming oysters brings out their subtle, briny taste and wonderful texture. Watch them carefully to prevent over-cooking. This dish is very simple to prepare and makes a dramatic opening for a special dinner party.

serves 4
preparation time: 20 minutes
cooking time: 10 minutes

16 large fresh oysters on the shell

Fresh coriander sprigs, to garnish

For the sauce:

2 teaspoons finely chopped garlic

1 tablespoon finely chopped fresh root ginger

1 teaspoon chilli bean sauce

1 tablespoon Shaoxing rice wine or dry sherry

1 tablespoon light soy sauce

2 teaspoons dark soy sauce

2 fresh red chillies, seeded and chopped

3 tablespoons finely shredded spring onions

3 tablespoons groundnut oil

1 Scrub the oysters clean. You will have to steam them in 2 batches, so divide them between 2 heatproof plates. Next set up a steamer or put a rack into a wok or deep pan and fill it with 5 cm (2 in) of water. Bring the water to the boil over a high heat. Put one plate of oysters into the steamer or on the rack, turn the heat to low and cover the wok or pan tightly. Steam the oysters gently for 5 minutes or until they are open.

2 Meanwhile, combine all the sauce ingredients except the groundnut oil in a heat-proof bowl.

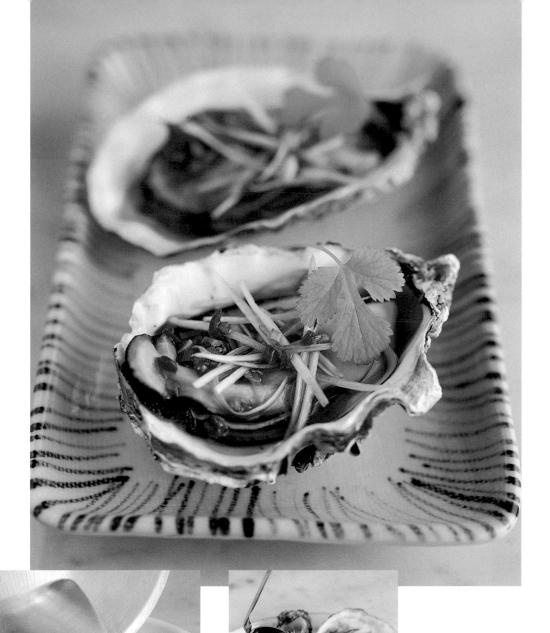

3 Heat a small pan over a high heat. Add the oil and, when it is very hot and slightly smoking, pour it over the sauce ingredients.

4 Remove the oysters from the steamer and cook the second batch. Give the sauce several good stirs. Remove the top shell of each oyster and pour a little sauce over the oysters. Garnish with coriander sprigs and serve.

MEAT and POULTRY

Stir-fried pork with spring onions

This recipe illustrates the relative ease of using a wok. A basic stir-fried meat dish can be made in minutes. The key to success here is not to overcook the pork.

serves 3–4
preparation time: 5 minutes, plus
    10–15 minutes' marinating
cooking time: 5–10 minutes

450 g (1 lb) lean boneless
    pork
1 tablespoon groundnut oil
8 spring onions, cut on the
    diagonal into 5 cm (2 in)
    lengths
1 teaspoon salt
½ teaspoon freshly ground
    black pepper
1 teaspoon sugar

For the marinade:
1 tablespoon Shaoxing rice
    wine or dry sherry
1 tablespoon light soy sauce
2 teaspoons sesame oil
1 teaspoon cornflour

1 Cut the pork into thin slices 5 cm (2 in) long.

2 Put the sliced pork into a bowl and mix in all the marinade ingredients. Leave for 10–15 minutes so that the pork absorbs the flavours of the marinade.

3 Heat a wok to a very high heat, then add the groundnut oil. When it is very hot and slightly smoking, add the pork slices and stir-fry for abour 2 minutes, until brown. Remove the meat with a slotted spoon and leave to drain in a colander.

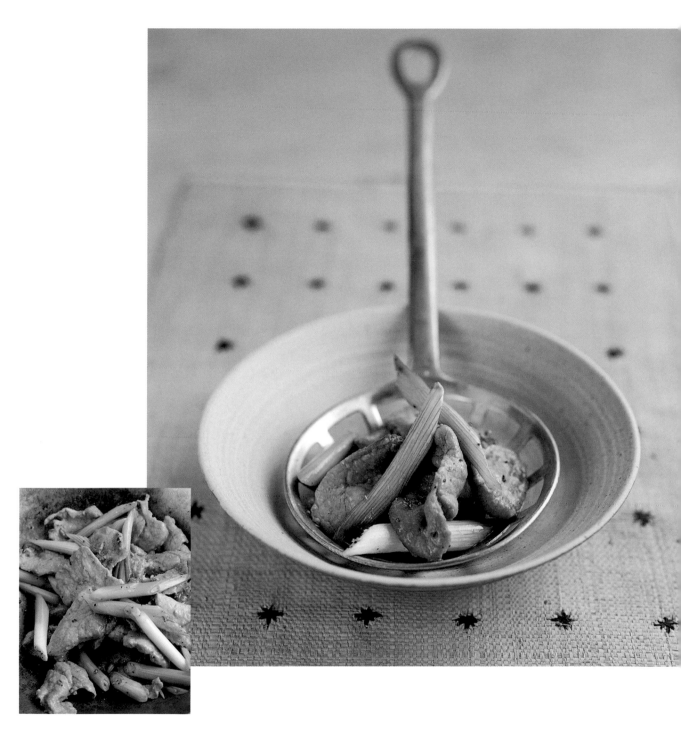

4 Reheat the wok and add the spring onions, salt, pepper and sugar. Stir-fry for 2 minutes or until the spring onions are wilted. Return the pork to the wok and stir-fry for another 2 minutes or until heated through. Serve at once.

Sweet and sour pork, Chiu Chow style

This delicious and unusual version of sweet and sour pork is based on a dish from a region of southern China. It is unlike most of the sweet and sour pork dishes offered in restaurants, which have become clichés bereft of their true character. Here, the minced pork is combined with crisp, sweet water chestnuts, seasoned and covered in caul fat. If you can't get caul fat, then just omit step 3 and dust the pork balls with the cornflour before deep-frying.

serves 4
preparation time: 35 minutes
cooking time: 15 minutes

450 g/1 lb minced fatty pork

1 egg white

4 tablespoons water

175 g/6 oz fresh or tinned water chestnuts, peeled if fresh, coarsely chopped

2 tablespoons light soy sauce

1 tablespoon dark soy sauce

2 tablespoons Shaoxing rice wine or dry sherry

1½ tablespoons sugar

2 teaspoons salt

½ teaspoon freshly ground black pepper

Caul fat for wrapping

100 g/4 oz carrots, thinly sliced on the diagonal

100 g/4 oz green pepper, cut into 2.5-cm (1-in) squares

100 g/4 oz red pepper, cut into 2.5 cm (1 in) squares

Cornflour for dusting

600 ml/1 pint groundnut oil

50 g/2 oz spring onions (about 4), cut into 2.5-cm (1-in) pieces

75 g/3 oz tinned lychees, drained, or fresh orange segments

For the sauce:

150 ml/5 fl oz *Classic Chinese chicken stock* (see page 26) or good-quality bought stock

1 tablespoon light soy sauce

2 teaspoons dark soy sauce

2 teaspoons sesame oil

½ teaspoon salt

½ teaspoon freshly ground white pepper

1½ tablespoons Chinese white rice vinegar or cider vinegar

1 tablespoon sugar

2 tablespoons tomato paste or tomato ketchup

2 teaspoons cornflour, blended with 1 tablespoon water

Fresh coriander leaves, to garnish (optional)

1 Mix the pork with the egg white and water, using your hand (this helps incorporate air). The mixture should be light and fluffy. Do not use a blender as it would make it too dense. Add the water chestnuts, light and dark soy sauce, rice wine or sherry, sugar, salt and pepper and mix thoroughly.

2 With your hands, shape the mixture into small rounds, about the size of golf balls.

3 Spread out the sheet of caul fat on a work surface and place the pork balls on it at 7.5-cm (3-in) intervals. Then cut the caul fat into 7.5-cm (3-in) squares and wrap it around each pork ball.

4 Bring a pan of water to the boil and blanch the carrots and peppers for about 4 minutes, until just tender. Drain and set aside.

5 Dust the pork balls with corn-flour, shaking off any excess. Heat the oil in a deep-fat fryer or large wok until slightly smoking. Reduce the heat to moderate and deep-fry the pork balls for 3–4 minutes, until crisp and cooked through. Remove with a slotted spoon and drain on kitchen paper.

6 In a large saucepan, combine all the sauce ingredients except the cornflour mixture and bring to the boil. Add the peppers, carrots and spring onions and stir well.
Stir in the cornflour mixture and cook for 2 minutes, then turn the heat down so that the mixture is simmering. Add the lychees or orange segments and the pork balls to the sauce. Mix well, then serve at once.

Crackling Chinese roast pork

One of the most fascinating sights in Chinatowns all over the world is shops with whole roast adult pigs as well as suckling pigs hanging in the window. The meat is delicious with rice or in stir-fried dishes. The secret of crispy skin is to blanch it and then let it dry using a technique similar to the one used for *Peking duck* (see page 90). Then the skin is slowly roasted so that most of fat runs off, leaving soft, tender pork flesh marbled with velvety fat. No wonder most diners are addicted to this delicious dish after the first bite. Much of the work can be done ahead of time and it is surprisingly easy.

serves 4–6
preparation time: 15 minutes,
    plus drying overnight
cooking time: 2½ hours

1.5 kg (3 lb) boneless pork
    belly, with rind

For the dry rub:

2 tablespoons coarse sea salt

1 tablespoon ground roasted
    Sichuan peppercorns (see
    page 15)

2 teaspoons five-spice
    powder

1 teaspoon freshly ground
    black pepper

2 teaspoons sugar

Perfect steamed rice to serve
    (optional, see page 110)

1 Pierce the rind side of the pork with a sharp fork or knife until the skin is covered with fine holes. Insert a meat hook into the pork.

2 Bring a large pan of water to the boil. Hang the pork up from the meat hook and, using a large ladle, pour the hot water over the rind side several times. Set the pork aside.

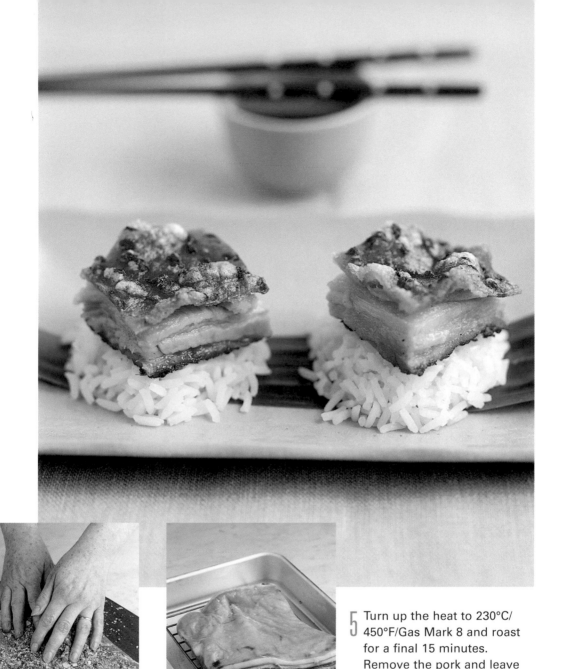

5 Turn up the heat to 230°C/ 450°F/Gas Mark 8 and roast for a final 15 minutes. Remove the pork and leave to cool. Then carve it into bite-sized pieces, arrange on a platter and serve. Alternatively, serve on beds of rice as shown.

3 Heat a wok, then add all the ingredients for the dry rub and stir-fry for 3 minutes until they are well mixed. Leave to cool slightly. When the dry rub is cool enough to handle, rub it all over the flesh side of the pork.

4 Hang the meat up to dry for 8 hours or overnight in a cool place or in front of a cold fan. Pre-heat the oven to 200°C/ 400°F/Gas Mark 6. Place the pork, rind side up, on a rack over a roasting tin of water. Roast for 15 minutes, then reduce the heat to 180°C/ 350°F/Gas Mark 4 and continue to roast for 2 hours.

Stir-fried beef with oyster sauce

This used to be one of the most popular dishes in my family's restaurant, especially with Westerners. It is very savoury and quite addictive. Buy the best brand of oyster sauce you can find. Good oyster sauce does not taste at all fishy. Rather, it has a meaty flavour and goes very well with beef or pork. This simple dish is delicious served with plain steamed rice.

450 g (1 lb) lean beef steak

1 tablespoon light soy sauce

2 teaspoons sesame oil

1 tablespoon Shaoxing rice wine or dry sherry

2 teaspoons cornflour

3 tablespoons groundnut oil

3 tablespoons oyster sauce

1½ tablespoons finely chopped spring onions, to garnish

serves 4
preparation time: 10 minutes, plus 20 minutes' marinating
cooking time: 10 minutes

1 Cut the beef into slices 5 cm (2 in) long and 5 mm (¼ in) thick, cutting against the grain of the meat. Put them into a bowl.

2 Mix in the soy sauce, sesame oil, rice wine or sherry and cornflour. Leave to marinate for 20 minutes.

3 Heat a wok until it is very hot, then add the groundnut oil. When it is very hot and slightly smoking, add the beef slices and stir-fry for 5 minutes or until lightly browned.

4 Remove the meat from the wok and drain well in a colander set inside a bowl. Discard the drained oil.

5 Wipe the wok clean and reheat it over a high heat. Add the oyster sauce and bring it to a simmer.

6 Return the drained beef slices to the wok and toss them thoroughly with the oyster sauce. Turn the mixture on to a serving platter, garnish with the spring onions and serve at once.

Stir-fried chicken with black bean sauce

This is a favourite of many first-time diners in Chinese restaurants, and no wonder. The fragrance of fermented black bean sauce mixed with garlic and ginger is mouthwatering. It can be cooked ahead of time and reheated, and it is also delicious served cold.

450 g (1 lb) boneless skinless chicken breasts, cut into 5 cm (2 in) chunks

1 tablespoon light soy sauce

1½ tablespoons Shaoxing rice wine or dry sherry

½ teaspoon salt

1 teaspoon sugar

1 teaspoon sesame oil

2 teaspoons cornflour

2 tablespoons groundnut oil

1 tablespoon finely chopped fresh root ginger

1½ tablespoons coarsely chopped garlic

2 tablespoons finely chopped shallots

3½ tablespoons finely chopped spring onions

2½ tablespoons coarsely chopped salted black beans

150 ml (5 fl oz) *Classic Chinese chicken stock* (see page 26) or good-quality bought stock

serves 4
preparation time: 15 minutes
cooking time: 10 minutes

1 Put the chicken in a bowl and mix with the soy sauce, rice wine or sherry, salt, sugar, sesame oil and cornflour.

2 Heat a wok over a high heat, then add the oil. When it is very hot and slightly smoking, add the chicken and stir-fry for 2 minutes.

3 Then add the ginger, garlic, shallots, 1½ tablespoons of the spring onions, and the black beans and stir-fry for 2 minutes.

4 Finally, add the stock. Bring the mixture to the boil, then reduce the heat, cover and simmer for 3 minutes or until the chicken is cooked. Garnish with the remaining spring onions and serve.

Spicy chicken with peanuts

This classic western Chinese dish is better known as *gongbao* or *kung pao* chicken. There are many versions of this recipe; this one is close to the original and is also easy to make.

serves 4
preparation time: 15 minutes
cooking time: 5–10 minutes

3 tablespoons groundnut oil

3 dried red chillies, split lengthways in half

450 g (1 lb) boneless skinless chicken breasts, cut into 2.5-cm (1-in) chunks

75 g (3 oz) roasted peanuts

For the sauce:

2 tablespoons *Classic Chinese chicken stock* (see page 26) or good-quality bought stock

2 tablespoons Shaoxing rice wine or dry sherry

1 tablespoon dark soy sauce

2 teaspoons sugar

1 tablespoon coarsely chopped garlic

2 teaspoons finely chopped spring onions

1 teaspoon finely chopped fresh root ginger

2 teaspoons Chinese white rice vinegar or cider vinegar

1 teaspoon salt

2 teaspoons sesame oil

1 Heat a wok over a high heat. Add the oil and chillies and stir-fry for a few seconds (you may remove the chillies when they turn black or leave them in).

2 Next add the chicken and peanuts and stir-fry for 1 minute. Remove the chicken, peanuts and chillies from the wok and drain in a colander.

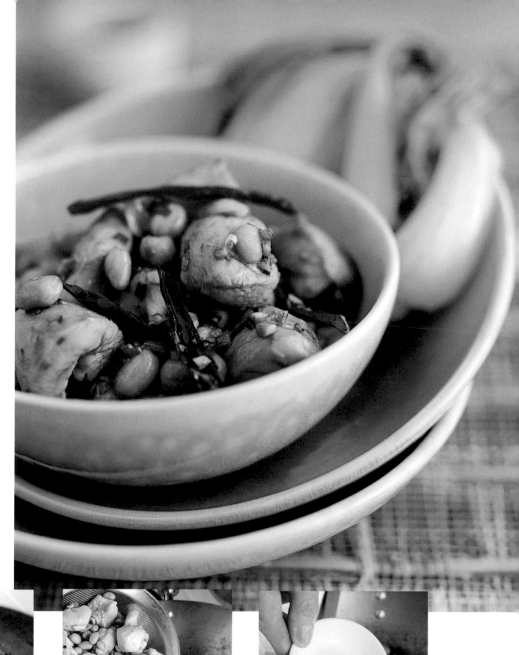

3 Put all the sauce ingredients except the sesame oil into the wok. Bring to the boil and then turn the heat down.

4 Return the chicken, peanuts and chillies to the wok and cook for about 3–4 minutes in the sauce, mixing well.

5 Finally, add the sesame oil, give the mixture a good stir, remove the chillies, if you prefer, and serve straight away.

Classic lemon chicken

The southern Chinese have made a speciality of chicken cooked with lemon. The tart sauce goes very well indeed with the receptive flavour of chicken. Unlike many versions, which employ a cloyingly sweet sauce, this recipe balances tartness with sweetness. Sometimes the lemon chicken is battered and deep-fried but I think it is equally good stir-fried, especially if the chicken is 'velveted' in hot oil or water beforehand.

serves 4
preparation time: 15 minutes, plus 20 minutes' chilling
cooking time: 10 minutes

450 g (1 lb) boneless, skinless chicken breasts, cut into strips 7.5 cm (3 in) long x 1 cm (½ in) thick

1 egg white

1 teaspoon salt

1 teaspoon sesame oil

2 teaspoons cornflour

300 ml (10 fl oz) groundnut oil or water

2 tablespoons finely chopped spring onions, to garnish

For the sauce:

65 ml (2½ fl oz) *Classic Chinese chicken stock* (see page 26) or good-quality bought stock

3 tablespoons fresh lemon juice

1 tablespoon sugar

1 tablespoon light soy sauce

1½ tablespoons Shaoxing rice wine or dry sherry

1½ tablespoons finely chopped garlic

1–2 teaspoons crushed dried red chilli

1 teaspoon cornflour, blended with 1 teaspoon water

2 teaspoons sesame oil

1 Put the chicken strips in a bowl and combine with the egg white, salt, sesame oil and cornflour. Put the mixture in the refrigerator for about 20 minutes.

2 If you are using oil for velveting the chicken, heat a wok until very hot and then add the oil. When it is very hot, remove the wok from the heat and immediately add the chicken, stirring vigorously to prevent it sticking. After about 2 minutes, when the chicken turns white, quickly drain it and all of the oil in a stainless steel colander set over a bowl. Discard the oil. If using water, do the same but bring the water to the boil in a saucepan before adding the chicken. It will take about 4 minutes to turn white in the water.

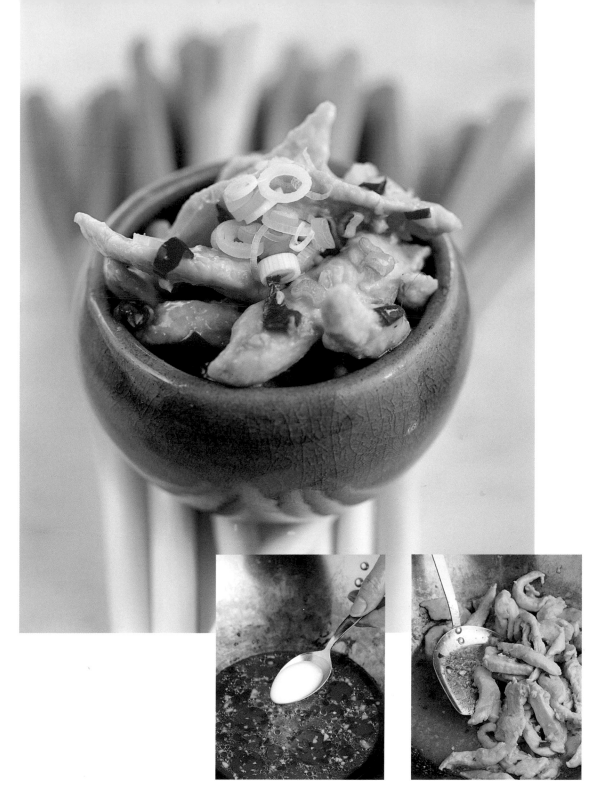

3 If you have used a wok, wipe it clean. Heat it, then add all the sauce ingredients except the cornflour mixture and sesame oil. Bring to a boil over a high heat and then add the cornflour mixture. Simmer for 1 minute.

4 Return the chicken strips to the wok and stir-fry long enough to coat them all with the sauce. Mix in the sesame oil, then turn on to a platter, garnish with the spring onions and serve at once.

Chinese chicken curry

Curry blends well with chicken, especially when used Chinese style as a light, subtle sauce that does not overpower the delicate taste of the meat. The chicken is 'velveted' before cooking to preserve its juiciness and flavour. You can do this by the traditional oil method or, for a less fattening dish, substitute water instead. This curry is mild, unlike traditional Indian curry.

> serves 4
> preparation time: 15 minutes, plus 20 minutes' chilling
> cooking time: 10 minutes

450 g (1 lb) boneless, skinless chicken breasts, cut into 2.5-cm (1-in) chunks

1 egg white

1 teaspoon salt

1 teaspoon sesame oil

3 teaspoons cornflour

300 ml (10 fl oz) groundnut oil or water

1 tablespoon groundnut oil

225 g (8 oz) red or green peppers, cut into 2.5-cm (1-in) pieces

1 tablespoon coarsely chopped garlic

150 ml (5 fl oz) *Classic Chinese chicken stock* (see page 26) or good-quality bought stock

1½ tablespoons Madras curry paste or powder

2 teaspoons sugar

1½ tablespoons Shaoxing rice wine or dry sherry

1½ tablespoons light soy sauce

1 teaspoon cornflour, blended with 1 tablespoon water

Fresh coriander leaves, to garnish (optional)

1 Put the chicken pieces in a bowl with the egg white, salt, sesame oil and 2 teaspoons of the cornflour and mix well. Put the mixture into the refrigerator for about 20 minutes.

2 If you are using oil for velveting the chicken, heat a wok until very hot and then add the oil. When it is very hot, remove the wok from the heat and immediately add the chicken, stirring vigorously to prevent it sticking. After about 2 minutes, when the chicken turns white, quickly drain it and all of the oil in a stainless steel colander set over a bowl. Discard the oil. If you are using water, do exactly the same but bring the water to the boil in a saucepan before adding the chicken. It will take about 4 minutes to turn white in the water.

3 If you have used the wok, wipe it clean. Heat it until it is very hot, then add the tablespoon of groundnut oil. When it is very hot, add the peppers and garlic and stir-fry for 2 minutes.

4 Add the stock, curry paste or powder, sugar, rice wine or sherry, soy sauce and cornflour mixture. Cook for 2 minutes. Add the drained chicken to the wok and stir-fry for another 2 minutes, coating the chicken thoroughly with the sauce. Serve at once.

Cashew chicken

This exemplifies the Chinese penchant for contrasting textures. Tender, succulent pieces of chicken are combined with sweet, crunchy cashew nuts. The secret to this popular dish is the use of that wonderful technique, velveting, in hot oil or water, which seals in the juices of the chicken, and then stir-frying as a second step to give it that special taste.

serves 4

preparation time: 10 minutes

cooking time: 5–10 minutes

450 g (1 lb) boneless, skin-less chicken breasts, cut into 1-cm (½-in) chunks

1 egg white

1 teaspoon salt

1 teaspoon sesame oil

2 teaspoons cornflour

300 ml (10 fl oz) groundnut oil or water

2 teaspoons groundnut oil

50 g (2 oz) cashew nuts

1 tablespoon Shaoxing rice wine or dry sherry

1 tablespoon light soy sauce

1 tablespoon finely shredded spring onions, to garnish

1 Put the chicken in a bowl with the egg white, salt, sesame oil and cornflour and mix well. Put the mixture in the refrigerator for about 20 minutes.

2 If you are using oil for velvet-ing the chicken, heat a wok until very hot and then add the oil. When it is very hot, remove the wok from the heat and immediately add the chicken, stirring vigorously to prevent it sticking. After about 2 minutes, when the chicken turns white, quickly drain it and all of the oil in a stainless steel colander set over a bowl. Discard the oil. If you are using water (as above), do exactly the same but bring the water to the boil in a saucepan before adding the chicken. It will take about 4 minutes to turn white in the water.

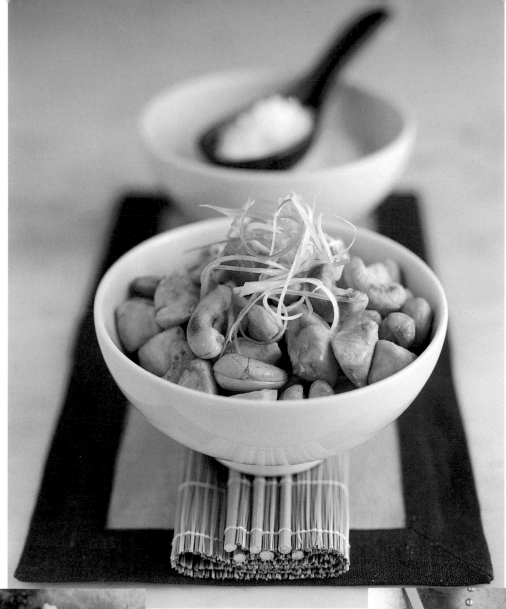

3 If you have used a wok, wipe it clean. Heat it until it is very hot, then add the 2 teaspoons of groundnut oil. Add the cashew nuts and stir-fry them for 1 minute.

4 Add the rice wine or dry sherry and soy sauce. Return the chicken to the wok and stir-fry for 2 minutes. Garnish with the spring onions and serve at once.

Peking duck

This is one of the most admired of all Chinese dishes. Certainly it is the one that captures everyone's fantasy of great Chinese food. How can one resist rich, succulent duck meat and crispy, crackling skin?

serves 4–6
preparation time: 20 minutes,
    plus at least 4 hours' drying
cooking time: 1½ hours

The classic preparation and cooking of Peking duck is an art form. Hot water combined with soy sauce and vinegar is poured over the duck to close the pores, then the bird is hung up to dry. During the drying process, a solution of malt sugar is liberally brushed over the duck, which is then roasted in wood-burning ovens. The result is a shiny, crisp, aromatic bird with beautiful brown skin, moist flesh and no fat.

Preparing Peking duck is a time-consuming task but I have devised a simpler method that gives impressive results, closely approximating the real thing. Just allow yourself plenty of time and the dish will be good enough for an emperor. If possible, use a plump, meaty duck, such as Cherry Valley, which is available from most large supermarkets.

Traditionally Peking duck is served with Chinese pancakes, shredded spring onions and sweet bean sauce. In Hong Kong and the West hoisin sauce is used instead. This is very similar to sweet bean sauce but contains vinegar. Each guest spoons some sauce on to a pancake, then places a helping of crisp skin and meat on top with some spring onion shreds and cucumber sticks. The entire mixture is rolled up in the pancake and then eaten using chopsticks or one's fingers. It makes an unforgettable dish for a special dinner party.

1 x 2.75 kg (6 lb) duck, fresh or frozen, preferably Cherry Valley

For the honey syrup:
2 tablespoons cider vinegar
1.2 litres (2 pints) water
3 tablespoons honey
3 tablespoons dark soy sauce

To serve:
Chinese pancakes (see page 106)
4 spring onions, finely shredded
1 cucumber, peeled, deseeded and cut into 5 x 2.5-cm (2 x 1-in) pieces
6 tablespoons hoisin sauce or sweet bean sauce

1 If the duck is frozen, thaw it thoroughly. Rinse it well and blot completely dry with kitchen paper. Insert a meat hook near the neck. Combine the ingredients for the honey syrup in a large wok or pan and bring to the boil. Holding the duck up by the meat hook, use a large ladle or spoon to pour the syrup over the duck several times, as if to bathe it, until the skin is completely coated with the mixture. Once used, the mixture can be discarded.

2 Hang the duck to dry in a cool, well-ventilated place, or hang it in front of a cold fan for about 4-5 hours, longer if possible. Be sure to put a tray or roasting tin underneath to catch any drips. Once the duck has dried, the skin will feel like parchment.

3 Pre-heat the oven to 240°C/475°F/Gas Mark 9. Place the duck, breast side up, on a roasting rack in a roasting tin. Put 150 ml (5 fl oz) of water into the tin (this will prevent the fat splattering). Now put the duck into the oven and roast it for 15 minutes. Turn the heat down to 180°C/350°F/Gas Mark 4 and continue to roast for 1 hour 10 minutes. Replenish the water as necessary.

4 Remove the duck from the oven and let it sit for at least 10 minutes before you carve it. Using a cleaver or a sharp knife, cut the skin and meat into pieces and arrange them on a warm platter. Serve at once, with the Chinese pancakes, spring onions, cucumber and a bowl of hoisin sauce or sweet bean sauce.

Crispy aromatic duck

This is probably one of the best-selling dishes in Chinese restaurants in the West. Although it is available as a ready-cooked meal, nothing beats the home-made version. Don't be intimidated by the long preparation process. Most of the steps are quite straightforward and can be done up to a day ahead, and the results are well worth the labour. Steaming the duck renders out most of the fat, leaving the meat moist and succulent. The final deep-frying crisps the skin beautifully.

serves 4–6
preparation time: 15 minutes, plus 2 hours' cooling
cooking time: 2½ hours

1 x 2.75 kg (6 lb) duck, fresh or frozen, preferably Cherry Valley

6 slices of fresh root ginger, 7.5 cm x 5 mm (3 x ¼ in)

6 spring onions, cut into 7.5-cm (3-in) lengths

Cornflour, plain flour or potato flour for dusting

1.2 litres (2 pints) groundnut oil

For the spice rub:

2 tablespoons five-spice powder

65 g (2½ oz) Sichuan peppercorns

25 g (1 oz) whole black peppercorns

3 tablespoons cumin seeds

200 g (7 oz) rock salt

To serve:

Chinese pancakes (see page 105)

6 spring onions, finely shredded

Hoisin sauce

1 If the duck is frozen, thaw it thoroughly. Rinse well and blot it completely dry with kitchen paper. Mix all the ingredients for the spice rub together in a small bowl, then rub the duck inside and out with this mixture, applying it evenly. Wrap well in clingfilm and place in the refrigerator for 24 hours.

2 After this time, brush any excess spices from the duck. Stuff the ginger and spring onions into the cavity and put the duck on a heatproof plate. Set up a steamer or put a rack into a wok. Fill it with 5 cm (2 in) of water and bring to the boil. Lower the duck and plate into the steamer and cover tightly.

3 Steam gently for 2 hours, pouring off excess fat from time to time. Add more water as necessary. Remove the duck from the steamer and pour off all the liquid. Discard the ginger and spring onions. Leave the duck in a cool place for 2 hours or until it has dried and cooled. At this point the duck can be refrigerated.

4 Just before you are ready to serve it, cut the duck into quarters and dust with corn-flour, plain flour or potato flour, shaking off the excess.

5 Heat the oil in a wok or deep-fat fryer. When it is almost smoking, deep-fry the duck quarters in 2 batches. Fry the breasts for about 8–10 min-utes and the thighs and legs for about 12–15 minutes, until each quarter is crisp and heated right through.

6 Drain the duck on kitchen paper and leave until cool enough to handle. Then remove the meat from the bones and shred it. You can do this easily with a fork. The Chinese eat it with bones and all. Serve with the Chinese pancakes, spring onions and hoisin sauce.

VEGETABLES and SIDE DISHES

Stir-fried spinach

This is a perfect way of cooking vegetables such as spinach that contain a great deal of moisture. The technique is to place the spinach in a very hot wok and quickly stir-fry with some seasoning. It is that simple to prepare, and may be served hot or cold.

675 g (1½ lb) fresh spinach
1 tablespoon groundnut oil
2 tablespoons coarsely
  chopped garlic

1 teaspoon salt
1 teaspoon sugar

serves 4
preparation time: 15 minutes
cooking time: 7 minutes

1 Wash the spinach thoroughly. Remove all the stems, leaving just the leaves.

2 Heat a wok over a high heat. Add the oil and, when it is very hot and slightly smoking, add the garlic and salt. Stir-fry for 10 seconds.

3 Add the spinach and stir-fry for about 2 minutes, until the leaves are thoroughly coated with the oil, garlic and salt.

4 When the spinach has wilted to about one-third of its original size, add the sugar and stir-fry for another 4 minutes. Transfer the spinach to a plate and pour off any excess liquid. Serve immediately.

Stir-fried broccoli

Stir-frying is one of the most appealing cooking techniques for this colourful and extraordinarily nutritious vegetable. The secret of making this simple dish is to add a little water and cover the wok tightly, so the broccoli can cook to perfection.

450 g (1 lb) broccoli

1½ tablespoons groundnut oil

4 garlic cloves, lightly crushed

1 teaspoon salt

½ teaspoon freshly ground black pepper

6 tablespoons water

2 teaspoons sesame oil

serves 4

preparation time: 10 minutes

cooking time: 6 minutes

1 Cut the stems off the broccoli and separate the heads into small florets. Peel and slice the stems.

2 Heat a wok over a high heat. Add the groundnut oil and, when it is very hot and slightly smoking, add the garlic, salt and pepper. Stir-fry for 30 seconds, or until the garlic is lightly browned.

3 Add the broccoli and stir-fry for 2 minutes. Now add the water, cover tightly and cook over a high heat for 4–5 minutes.

4 Uncover and test the broccoli by gently piercing it with the tip of a sharp knife; it should go in quite easily. Stir in the sesame oil and stir-fry for 30 seconds, then serve.

Stir-fried mixed vegetables

Stir-fried vegetable dishes should not contain more than four or five types of vegetable and they should be varied – some crisp, like green beans, others leafy, such as spinach. The art of stir-frying vegetables is knowing when to add them to the wok. If you throw them all in at once they can become soggy, regardless of their water content. Put the tougher, more textured ones in the wok first to give them a head start. The amount of cooking water you need to add depends on how much natural water is in the vegetables you are using. Make sure you add only the minimum amount (no more than 1–2 tablespoons) if you are using the wok covered, otherwise the vegetables will over steam and become soggy.

serves 4
preparation time: 15 minutes
cooking time: 7 minutes

225 g (8 oz) Chinese leaves
  (Peking cabbage)

225 g (8 oz) Chinese greens,
  such as Chinese flowering
  cabbage or pak choy, or
  spinach

225 g (8 oz) asparagus

225 g (8 oz) carrots

1½ tablespoons groundnut oil

2 tablespoons coarsely
  chopped shallots

2 tablespoons coarsely
  chopped garlic

2 teaspoons finely chopped
  fresh root ginger

2 teaspoons salt

1–2 tablespoons water

2 teaspoons sugar

1 tablespoon Shaoxing rice
  wine or dry sherry

2 teaspoons sesame oil

1 Cut the Chinese leaves into 4-cm (1½-in) strips. Then cut the greens and asparagus into 4-cm (1½-in) pieces. Cut the carrots on the diagonal into slices 5 mm (¼ in) thick.

2 Heat a wok over a high heat. Add the groundnut oil and, when it is very hot and slightly smoking, add the shallots, garlic, ginger and salt and stir-fry for 1 minute.

3 Then add the carrots and asparagus and stir-fry for 30 seconds. Add the water, cover and cook over a high heat for 2 minutes.

4 Add the Chinese leaves and greens, together with the sugar and rice wine or sherry. Stir-fry for 3 minutes or until the greens are thoroughly wilted. Then add the sesame oil and serve at once.

Braised Sichuan-style spicy beancurd

This traditional dish from Sichuan province in China is becoming popular in the West. Bland but very healthy bean-curd is mixed with spicy, fragrant ingredients to produce a sensational dish that is simply mouthwatering. The essence of this recipe lies with the quality of the seasonings and condiments and the care taken in cooking them just right.

serves 4
preparation time: 5 minutes
cooking time: 6 minutes

450 g (1 lb) fresh beancurd
1 tablespoon groundnut oil
1 tablespoon whole yellow bean sauce
1 tablespoon dark soy sauce
½ teaspoon salt
1 teaspoon red chilli powder or cayenne pepper, or to taste

175 ml (6 fl oz) *Classic Chinese chicken stock* (see page 26) or good-quality bought stock
2 tablespoons coarsely chopped garlic
2 teaspoons cornflour, mixed with 1 tablespoon water
1 teaspoon finely ground roasted Sichuan pepper-corns (see page 15)

1 Gently cut the beancurd into 4-cm (1½-in) cubes.

2 Heat a wok, add the ground-nut oil and yellow bean sauce and stir-fry for 30 seconds. Add the soy sauce and salt and stir-fry for 1 minute.

3 Add the chilli powder and stir-fry for 30 seconds. Then pour in the stock, add the beancurd and simmer for 3 minutes.

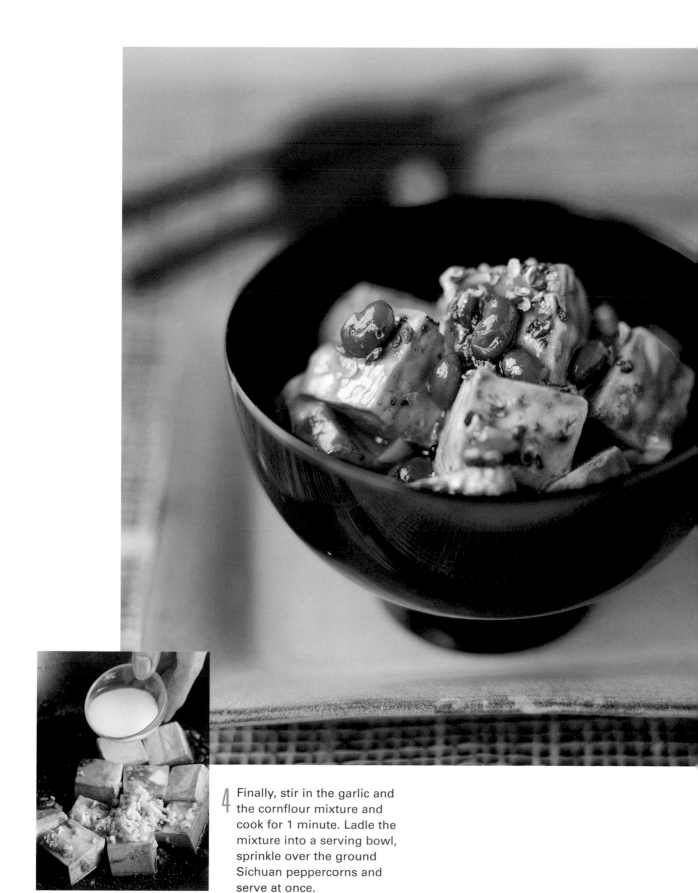

4 Finally, stir in the garlic and the cornflour mixture and cook for 1 minute. Ladle the mixture into a serving bowl, sprinkle over the ground Sichuan peppercorns and serve at once.

Sichuan-style green beans

This delectable dish originated in western China, as its seasonings indicate. The traditional recipe calls for Chinese asparagus or long beans but I find green beans equally suitable. They are deep-fried to give them a soft rather than a crunchy texture but they should remain green and not be overcooked. After deep-frying, the beans are stir-fried in an array of spices. They should be slightly oily but if they are too oily for your taste you can blot them with kitchen paper before stir-frying them. For best results, serve the beans as soon as they are cooked. A delicious vegetarian dish.

serves 4
preparation time: 10 minutes
cooking time: 10 minutes

600 ml (1 pint) groundnut oil

450 g (1 lb) green beans, sliced if long; left whole otherwise

2 tablespoons coarsely chopped garlic

1 tablespoon finely chopped fresh root ginger

3 tablespoons finely chopped spring onions (white part only)

1½ tablespoons chilli bean sauce

1 tablespoon whole yellow bean sauce

2 tablespoons Shaoxing rice wine or dry sherry

1 tablespoon dark soy sauce

2 teaspoons sugar

1 tablespoon water

2 teaspoons chilli oil

1 Heat a wok over a high heat. Add the oil and, when it is very hot and slightly smoking, deep-fry half the beans until slightly wrinkled, which should take about 3–4 minutes. Remove the beans and drain them. Deep-fry the second batch in the same way.

2 Transfer about 1 tablespoon of the oil in which you have cooked the beans to a clean wok or frying-pan. Heat the oil, then add the garlic, ginger and spring onions and stir-fry for 30 seconds.

3 Add all the rest of the ingredients except the green beans and stir-fry for 30 seconds.

4 Add the drained beans and mix until they are thoroughly coated with the spicy mixture. Serve as soon as the beans have heated through.

Chinese pancakes

These pancakes are the classic accompaniment to Peking Duck (see page 90) and Crispy Aromatic Duck (see page 92) and reflect the northern Chinese use of wheat instead of rice. They are easy to make once you get the knack, which comes with practice. The unusual method of rolling 'double' pancakes is designed to ensure thinner, moister pancakes with less risk of overcooking them. Since they can be frozen, wrapped tightly in clingfilm, it is possible to make them weeks ahead.

To reheat the pancakes, steam them briefly, or you could cover them tightly with clingfilm and microwave them – this takes only a minute. Don't be tempted to reheat them in the oven as this will dry them out too much. When using pancakes that have been frozen, let them thaw in the refrigerator before reheating.

serves 6–8
preparation time: 40 minutes, plus 30 minutes' resting the dough
cooking time: 20–30 minutes

275 g (10 oz) plain flour, plus extra for dusting
250 ml (8 fl oz) very hot water
2 tablespoons sesame oil

1 Put the flour into a large bowl. Gradually stir in the hot water, mixing all the while with chopsticks or a fork until it is fully incorporated. Add more water if the mixture seems dry.

2 Turn the dough out and knead it with your hands for about 8 minutes or until it is smooth, dusting with flour if necessary, as it may be quite sticky at this point. Put the dough back into the bowl, cover it with a damp tea-towel and let it rest for about 30 minutes.

3 Remove the dough from the bowl and knead it again for about 5 minutes, dusting with a little flour if it is sticky. Once the dough is smooth, form it into a roll about 45 cm (18 in) long and 2.5 cm (1 in) thick. Cut the roll into 18 equal pieces and shape each one into a ball.

4 Take 2 of the dough balls. Dip one side of one ball into the sesame oil and place the oiled side on top of the other ball.

7 Right: Remove from the pan and let it cool slightly. When it is still warm, but cool enough to handle, peel the 2 pancakes apart and set them aside. Repeat this process until all the dough balls have been cooked.

5 With a rolling pin, roll the 2 pancakes simultaneously into a circle about 15 cm (6 in) in diameter. You can flip the double pancake over and roll on the other side as well.

6 Heat a frying-pan or wok over a very low flame. Put the double pancake into the pan and cook it for 1–2 minutes, until it has dried underneath; there may be brown specks. Flip it over and cook the other side until dried as well.

Perfect steamed rice

The Chinese way of steaming rice is simple, direct and effective. I prefer to use long-grain white rice, which is dry and fluffy when cooked. Don't use pre-cooked or 'easy-cook' rice as it lacks the texture and starchy taste fundamental to Chinese rice.

The secret of preparing rice without it becoming sticky is to cook it first in an uncovered pan at a high heat until most of the water has evaporated. Then the heat should be turned very low, the pan covered and the rice cooked slowly in the remaining steam. Never uncover the pan once the steaming process has begun; just time it and wait.

Here is a good trick to remember: if you cover the rice with about 2.5 cm (1 in) of water it should always cook properly without sticking. Many packet recipes for rice use too much water and result in a gluey mess. Follow my method and you will have perfect steamed rice, the easy Chinese way.

serves 4
preparation time: 20 minutes
cooking time: 20 minutes

Enough long-grain rice to fill a glass measuring jug to 400 ml (14 fl oz)

600 ml (1 pint) water

3 At this point, cover the pan with a very tight-fitting lid, turn the heat as low as possible and let the rice cook undisturbed for 15 minutes. There is no need to 'fluff' the rice; just let it rest off the heat for 5 minutes before serving.

1 Put the rice into a large bowl and wash it in several changes of water until the water becomes clear.

2 Drain the rice. Put in a heavy pan with the 600 ml (1 pint) water and bring to the boil. Boil for about 5 minutes until most of the surface liquid has evaporated. The surface of the rice should have small indentations like a pitted crater.

Egg-fried rice

Egg fried rice is common in Chinese restaurants and is probably the best-known Chinese dish in the West. The secret is to use cold cooked rice and a very hot wok. Remember that authentic fried rice should have a wonderful smoky taste, and should never be greasy or heavy.

serves 4
preparation time: 5 minutes
cooking time: 8 minutes

2 large eggs, lightly beaten

2 teaspoons sesame oil

1 teaspoon salt

2 tablespoons groundnut oil

1 quantity of *Perfect steamed rice* (see page 110), cooled completely

¼ teaspoon freshly ground black pepper

2 tablespoons finely chopped spring onions

3 Next drizzle in the egg and oil mixture and continue to stir-fry for 2–3 minutes or until the eggs have set and the mixture is dry.

4 Add the remaining salt and the pepper and stir-fry for 2 minutes longer, then toss in the spring onions. Stir several times, turn on to a platter and serve at once.

1 Put the eggs, sesame oil and half the salt in a small jug or bowl, mix with a fork and set aside.

2 Heat a wok over a high heat. Add the groundnut oil and, when it is very hot and slightly smoking, add the cold cooked rice. Stir-fry for 3 minutes, or until it is thoroughly heated through.

Chow mein

Chow mein literally means 'stir-fried noodles' and this dish is as popular in the West as it is in southern China. It is a quick and delicious way to prepare egg noodles. Almost any ingredient you like, such as fish, meat, poultry or vegetables, can be added to it. It makes a popular lunch dish, either served at the end of the meal or eaten by itself.

serves 4
preparation time: 10 minutes,
    plus 10 minutes' marinating
cooking time: 20 minutes

225 g (8 oz) dried or fresh egg noodles

4 teaspoons sesame oil

100 g (4 oz) boneless, skinless chicken breasts, cut into fine shreds 5 cm (2 in) long

2½ tablespoons groundnut oil

1 tablespoon finely chopped garlic

50 g (2 oz) mangetout, finely shredded

50 g (2 oz) Parma ham or cooked ham, finely shredded

2 teaspoons light soy sauce

2 teaspoons dark soy sauce

1 tablespoon Shaoxing rice wine or dry sherry

1 teaspoon salt

½ teaspoon freshly ground white pepper

½ teaspoon sugar

3 tablespoons finely chopped spring onions

For the marinade:

2 teaspoons light soy sauce

2 teaspoons Shaoxing rice wine or dry sherry

1 teaspoon sesame oil

½ teaspoon salt

½ teaspoon freshly ground white pepper

1 Cook the noodles in a large pan of boiling water for 3–5 minutes, then drain and plunge them in cold water. Drain thoroughly, toss them with 3 teaspoons of the sesame oil and set aside.

2 Combine the chicken shreds with all the marinade ingredients, mix well and then leave to marinate for about 10 minutes.

3 Heat a wok over a high heat. Add 1 tablespoon of the groundnut oil and, when it is very hot and slightly smoking, add the chicken shreds. Stir-fry for about 2 minutes and then transfer to a plate. Wipe the wok clean.

4 Reheat the wok until it is very hot, then add the remaining groundnut oil. When the oil is slightly smoking, add the garlic and stir-fry for 10 seconds. Then add the mangetout and ham and stir-fry for about 1 minute.

5 Left: Add the noodles, soy sauces, rice wine or sherry, salt, pepper, sugar and spring onions. Stir-fry for 2 minutes.

6 Return the chicken and any juices to the noodle mixture. Stir-fry for about 3–4 minutes or until the chicken is cooked.

7 Add the remaining sesame oil and give the mixture a few final stirs. Turn it on to a warm platter and serve at once.

Northern-style cold noodles

These savoury noodles are perfect for any meal or snack. They are quick and easy to make but if you wish to prepare them ahead of time, keep the sauce and noodles separate until the last possible moment.

serves 4
preparation time: 10 minutes
cooking time: 3–5 minutes

350 g (12 oz) dried or fresh
   egg noodles
2 tablespoons sesame oil
3 tablespoons finely chopped
   spring onions, to garnish

For the sauce:
3 tablespoons sesame paste
   or peanut butter
1½ tablespoons finely
   chopped garlic
2 teaspoons finely chopped
   fresh root ginger
2 teaspoons chilli bean sauce
3 tablespoons Chinese white
   vinegar or cider vinegar
2 tablespoons orange juice
2 tablespoons light soy sauce
2 teaspoons dark soy sauce
½ teaspoon salt
½ teaspoon freshly ground
   black pepper
2 teaspoons sugar
2 teaspoons ground roasted
   Sichuan peppercorns (see
   page 15)
1 tablespoon groundnut oil
1½ tablespoons sesame oil

1 Cook the noodles in a large pan of boiling water for 3–5 minutes, then drain and plunge them in cold water.

2 Drain the noodles thoroughly and toss them with the sesame oil. Arrange them on a platter or in a large bowl.

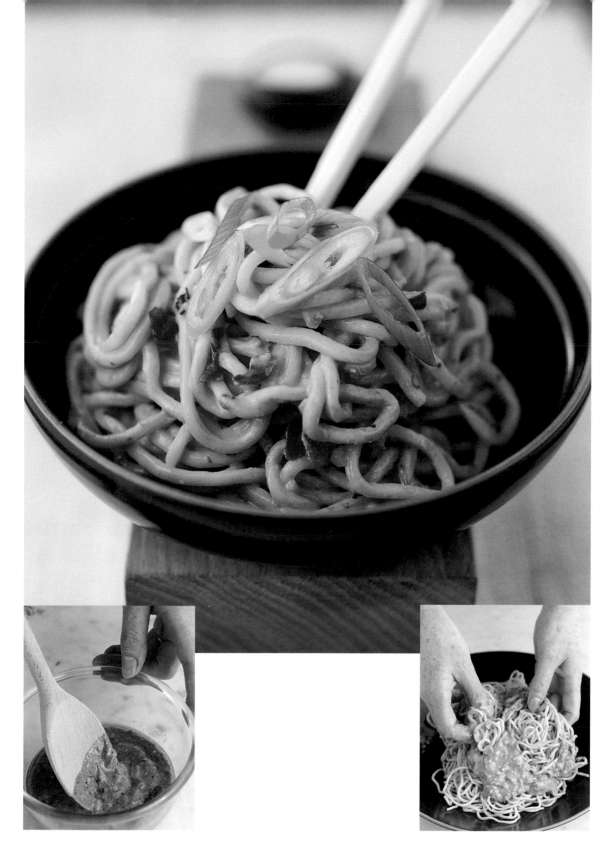

3 The sauce can be made in advance and kept refrigerated, as it is served cold. Just mix all the ingredients together in a bowl or an electric blender.

4 When ready to serve, pour the sauce on top of the noodles and toss well, then garnish with the spring onions.

Singapore noodles

This is the ultimate Fusion noodle dish. Curry is not original to Chinese cuisine. It was introduced to China centuries ago by immigrants returning home from sojourns in Southeast Asia, especially from the east coast of India. This is why even today curry continues to be popular in southern and eastern China, where many immigrants returned from faraway Singapore. Chinese cuisine readily adopts new foods and ingredients when their virtues are recognized. These light and subtle rice noodles make an ideal foil for the spicy sauce.

serves 6–8
preparation time: 20 minutes, plus 25 minutes' soaking
cooking time: 15 minutes

225 g (8 oz) thin dried rice noodles

2 eggs, beaten

1 tablespoon sesame oil

1 teaspoon salt

½ teaspoon freshly ground black pepper

3 tablespoons groundnut oil

1½ tablespoons coarsely chopped garlic

1 tablespoon finely chopped fresh root ginger

6 fresh red or green chillies, seeded and finely shredded

6 fresh or tinned water chest-nuts, peeled if fresh, sliced

50 g (2 oz) Chinese black mushrooms, soaked, stems removed (see page 11) and finely shredded

100 g (4 oz) Chinese barbe-cue pork or cooked ham, finely shredded

3 spring onions, finely shredded

100 g (4 oz) cooked small prawns, shelled

175 g (6 oz) small, sweet frozen peas, thawed

Fresh coriander leaves, to garnish

For the curry sauce:

2 tablespoons light soy sauce

3 tablespoons Indian Madras curry paste or powder

2 tablespoons Shaoxing rice wine or dry sherry

1 tablespoon sugar

1 teaspoon salt

1 teaspoon freshly ground black pepper

250 ml (8 fl oz) tinned coconut milk

175 ml (6 fl oz) *Classic Chinese chicken stock* (see page 26) or good-quality bought stock

1 Soak the rice noodles in a bowl of warm water for 25 minutes, then drain them in a colander or sieve. In a small bowl, combine the eggs with the sesame oil, salt and pepper and set aside.

2 Heat a wok over a high heat, then add the groundnut oil. When it is very hot and slightly smoking, add the garlic, ginger and chillies and stir-fry for 30 seconds.

3 Add the water chestnuts, mushrooms, pork or ham and spring onions and stir-fry for 1 minute. Then add the rice noodles, prawns and peas and stir-fry for another 2 minutes.

4 Add all the sauce ingredients and cook over a high heat for 5 minutes or until most of the liquid has evaporated.

5 Now pour the egg mixture over the noodles and stir-fry constantly until the egg has set. Turn the noodles on to a large platter, garnish with coriander leaves and serve at once.

Menus

Here is some simple advice on how to put together a Chinese meal, plus suggested menus for a variety of occasions. Start with some of the easy ones, which will give you experience of the basic cooking techniques. At first, cook just one or two Chinese dishes at a time, perhaps including them as part of a European meal. Chinese snacks, for example, make wonderful starters at any meal, and many Chinese dishes can successfully be combined with Western-style meats and salads.

When you prepare your first completely Chinese meal, choose just two or three dishes and serve them with some plain steamed rice. Never select dishes that all need stir-frying or you will have a traumatic time in the kitchen trying to get everything ready at once and will arrive at the table hot and flustered. Choose instead one braised dish, a cold dish, or something that can be prepared ahead of time then warmed through, and limit your stir-frying to just one dish. This means that not only will you gain the confidence needed to try more ambitious recipes but also your meal will be all the more authentic for embracing a variety of techniques.

Remember that the art of Chinese cooking lies in achieving a harmonious blend of colour, texture, aroma and flavour. This involves using a range of cooking methods. A fish may be steamed, a meat braised, while the vegetables may be stir-fried. A meal will also be designed so that each dish is different and yet they all complement each other. One dish will be spicy and another mild; one may be chewy, another crisp. The total effect should appeal to all the senses. All the dishes should be placed in the centre of the table and shared between the diners, who help themselves and each other to a little of this and then a little of that. For the Chinese, eating is a communal experience, and a shared meal is regarded as the visible manifestation of the harmony that should exist between family and friends.

Dinner Party for 6

This is an elegant, stylish meal for friends. It is quite ambitious but much of the work can be done ahead of time. Both the soup and the rice can be reheated. Serve the soup first, followed by the prawns, then serve the duck and rice. Increase the quantities given in the recipes by half to serve six.

Sweetcorn and crab soup

Spicy Sichuan-style prawns

Crispy aromatic duck

Egg-fried rice

Dinner Party for 6

This is a simpler menu than the one on page 123 and is light and tasty. Serve the fish first, followed by the chicken with spinach and rice. Increase the quantities given in the recipes by half to serve six.

Steamed Cantonese-style fish

Stir-fried chicken with black bean sauce

Stir-fried spinach

Perfect steamed rice

Dinner Party for 6

Here is a savoury treat for your vegetarian friends. There is a variety of textures and tastes in this easy-to-prepare meal. Substitute vegetable stock for the chicken stock in the *Braised Sichuan-style spicy beancurd*. Increase the quantities given in the recipes by half to serve six.

Crispy 'seaweed'

Stir-fried mixed vegetables

Braised Sichuan-style spicy beancurd

Perfect steamed rice

Buffet for 20

This is a very manageable feast for 20. Much of the preparation can be done hours beforehand, leaving you free to enjoy your own party. I have suggested quantities for each recipe, but this will depend on your guests' appetite!

Sesame prawn toast

(double the recipe quantity)

Peking-style caramel walnuts

(make four times the recipe quantity)

Crispy fried wontons

(make five times the recipe quantity)

Cashew chicken

(make five times the recipe quantity)

Spring rolls

(double the recipe quantity)

Northern-style cold noodles

(make five times the recipe quantity)

Family Meal for 4

A healthy and nutritious meal
for your family.

Sweet and sour pork, Chiu Chow style

Stir-fried broccoli

Chow mein

Romantic Dinner for 2

An effortless meal that leaves time for
talking – the essence of a romantic dinner.
Serve the dishes one at a time so you can
linger over your meal. Halve the quantities
given in the recipes to serve two.

Cantonese egg flower soup

Steamed fresh oysters

Stir-fried pork with spring onions

Perfect steamed rice

Index